*Climbing Plants
and some Wall Shrubs*

CLIMBING PLANTS

AND SOME
WALL SHRUBS

by

Douglas Bartrum

THE GARDEN BOOK CLUB
121 CHARING CROSS ROAD
LONDON, W.C.2

First published 1959
This revised edition 1968
© *Douglas Bartrum* 1959

Printed in Great Britain by offset lithography
by Billing & Sons Limited, Guildford and London

CONTENTS

LIST OF ILLUSTRATIONS

LINE DRAWINGS

LIST OF ILLUSTRATIONS

INTRODUCTION

[1]

W E may divide ornamental climbers into three groups. Those we grow specially for their flowers – like Honeysuckle (usually the scented varieties) and Clematis. Those that have attractive foliage but little floral beauty. And the winter-berrying kinds.

The Climbing Roses and the large-flowered Clematis would be chosen no doubt by most people in preference to, say, the Virginia Creeper, though this is a lovely plant in the autumn, with its scarlet and yellow leaves. Brilliantly-coloured foliage attracts us almost as much as flowers.

The foliage seldom lasts as long, however (it often falls overnight after a severe frost), and it lacks the fragrance of the flowers of many climbers. If these happen to be fragrant as well as showy, then the plants are doubly valuable; and, extending the virtues, if they have leaves and berries which colour well in autumn and winter, we could wish for nothing more.

The Common Honeysuckle has red berries, but they are not particularly decorative, and of course it is not for them that we grow the plant. It is lovely in full bloom but by no means as showy as many of the garden Clematis. It is primarily for its scent that we plant it. Gardeners who have grown the Chinese species, *Lonicera tragophylla*, with yellow trumpet flowers, are usually surprised and disappointed to find that these are scentless. In fact, I have known several gardeners who have dug it up and planted the purple Clematis (*C.* × *Jackmanii*) in its place.

9

Climbers can be grown in many ways. On walls, arches, fences, crude wooden supports and trellis-work. On trees and shrubs: those we choose being usually of little value: they are often dead or on their last legs. Pergolas and arbours are meant to be covered or partly covered with climbers. And the most uncommon, the most unorthodox way, is that of allowing them to ramble freely over the ground. They cease then to be climbers and become perforce 'spreaders' or creepers. Some Clematis are grown in this way at Kew Botanic Gardens. The more tender kinds are often grown in pots and housed during the winter – they can be stood outside in the summer. Where a cool greenhouse is available, they are best planted out in prepared beds against one of the walls and allowed to grow much as they would in the open, provided, of course, that there is the necessary space. If they are grown in pots and space is limited, a single support such as a bamboo cane or a tall, twiggy branch is all that can be used. Clematis are usually sent out in pots and have a single cane about 3 feet tall to support them; they may be grown in this way for several years and make most attractive pot plants. True, they are a little tall for tables and window-sills, but they are ideal for standing on the floor of an entrance hall.

Many climbers are used for indoor decoration: in large centre-pieces for tables, side-boards, etc., and in bouquets. A trail of Clematis is very effective among sprays of flowering shrubs and perennial border plants. Ivy leaves and vine leaves are an excellent foil to many flowers.

[2]

THE most popular climbers are easy to grow and flourish practically anywhere in this country. (With 'Climbers' I class twiners and lax, shrubby plants like the yellow Winter Jasmine). *Clematis*, Climbing Roses, Jasmine (*Jasminum*), Honeysuckle (*Lonicera*) and *Wistaria* are probably the five favourite families. We see them more often than any other climbing plants, and most nurseries have them for sale.

If I had to name the three most popular of all the many

species and varieties included in these five families, I should say the yellow Winter Jasmine (*J. nudiflorum*), the fragrant, white summer species *J. officinale*, and the purple *Clematis* × *Jackmanii*. The last is seen more often, I believe, than the common, fragrant Honeysuckle – perhaps because on the whole it is easier to grow. These three thrive in any ordinary garden soil.

Clematis need lime: it is a simple matter to dig in lime-rubble round the roots at the time of planting. (I prefer to add it even in naturally limy soils.)

Garden varieties of the Climbing Roses need loamy soil, but some of the species of Wild Roses do best in quite poor, sandy ground.

The yellow Winter Jasmine will grow in almost any garden; so will the fragrant summer variety *J. officinale*.

The common Honeysuckle (Woodbine) and Wistaria do well in ordinary soil, provided it never dries out. The finest specimens will be found planted in moist loams.

Every gardener would like to grow something rarer than these climbers, however. And there is, of course, a wide choice, though not all would be called 'rare' by everybody. Those that are seldom seen around London and farther up country may be common enough in Cornwall and in other warm maritime districts. The Daisy Climber, *Mutisia decurrens* from Chile, flourishes in the south but is rarely seen in northern gardens. Its tenderness makes it rare. Nonetheless it may be tried against a wall and, if given protection during the winter, will prove a success.

Hydrangea petiolaris (the Climbing Hydrangea) on the other hand is hardy but rare, probably because it needs so much room. It is a climber for a large garden: it wants a big tree or a high wall on which to display itself. There are many others that we can place in the same class: they are perforce rarities in most districts but are fairly widely grown where the climate is suitable.

What we might call genuine rarities are those that are too tender for outdoor cultivation in these islands and consequently have to be housed. The beautiful, blue *Plumbago capensis* from South Africa needs a cool greenhouse. Perhaps *Lapageria rosea*, the Bell Climber, should be similarly accommodated although it flowers well out of doors in Devon and Cornwall. The Wild Rose *Rosa gigantea*, originally found in Upper Burma, is regarded as the most striking of all the rose species; it has fragrant yellow flowers about 6 inches across and will climb up 70 feet or more in warm climates: a climber all of us would like to possess. It is a magnificent sight in the Temperate House at Kew Botanic Gardens. Plants such as these are the rare climbers of our gardens. Attempts have been made to grow them, or some of them, outside; but it hardly seems worth the trouble in most districts: without a greenhouse, it is best to leave them alone.

Climbing or trailing plants that are grown in pots for indoor decoration are usually tender. *Hedera canariensis* (the Canary Island Ivy) is – a charming foliage climber for a pot. Others, however, like the decorative varieties of the Common Ivy, are hardy. As a rule these plants do not grow very tall and, as I have already stated, some are of trailing habit. More often than not they are grown for their uncommonly beautiful foliage.

Shrubs which may or may not be tender are sometimes grown against a wall – tender ones like the Ceanothus from California need a wall. Camellias, too, flower more freely when planted near a wall. And probably all the winter-blooming shrubs ought to be planted against warm, sheltered walls. The bright yellow *Forsythia suspensa* does best there, its long rambling branches being easily trained up to a good height. I have seen it in full bloom in January.

Another is the November-blooming *Viburnum fragrans*, which in the open garden makes a roundish bush up to 10 feet high. On a wall it may be trained, with its branches spread out, rather in the form of an espalier (as it is at Kew) and will reach a height of 15 feet or more and as much wide. This is not its normal shape, of course: pruning is necessary to keep it shapely and tidy. I have never come across a specimen so full of blossom as the one at Kew; it is at its best about mid-November; and the rich heavy scent of its flowers is perceptible a good distance away.

[3]

GROWN and trained in this way, the shrub assumes the appearance of a large, woody climber. The main trunk and the spreading branches in close proximity to the brickwork lose their roundness and become flat. Other conditions under which a shrub grows can have a different influence on its character. If, for example, several are planted close together in deep shade, they quickly become tall and lanky. A rooted cutting of the common *Euonymus japonicus* planted in a Laurel hedge to fill a gap will often form a single, slender stem with etiolated leaves instead of growing into a bush, and only produce its normal, thick, dark glossy green leaves when the stem has topped the hedge and finally reached the sunlight. In fact, we might say that the *Euonymus* has assumed the character of a climber.

In the *Botanical Magazine* (t, 3948) the Brazilian Fuchsia (*F. integrifolia*) is described; the remarks there by a Mr. Gardner, who saw it in the wild, are of special interest, as they reveal the influence of environment on the habits of certain plants. "The plant is very common in the Organ Mountains. I have not met with it lower than 3,000 feet above the elevation of the sea, but from that altitude, to about 6,000 feet, it abounds. In the Virgin forests it is most common by the sides of streams, climbing up the stems of the large trees, and flowering among the branches. I have seen it reach to a height of 40 or 50 feet, giving the trees to which it has attached itself the appearance of being Fuchsias themselves. At an elevation of 5–6,000 feet it loses its climbing habit and becomes a bush, varying from 2 to 4 feet high." The Lianas of South America adapt themselves similarly to their environment: those that grow in open places – for instance, on sunny, rocky ground – are of bush habit; those within the forests become climbers. Very probably the climbing forms are derived from the bushes. And no doubt many climbers originated in the deep shade of forests, the plants first growing erect and along the lower branches of trees and finally moving upward in search of the light.

The common Periwinkle, normally an erect or semi-trailing

herbaceous plant, will climb if grown in a pot and given a support (say, a Beech twig) and left in a dark room; the Broad Bean behaves similarly. I have twisted the long stem of the Periwinkle (*Vinca major*) which has been growing in deep shade, round a support, but the stem needed tying to keep it in position. With most plants that twist and twine naturally, this of course is not necessary. We may cite the common Honeysuckle (*Lonicera periclymenum*), which flourishes luxuriantly in our hedgerows and goes up to a height of 20 feet or more. The Japanese evergreen species *L. japonica* is another; and this plant is particularly interesting in its habit of producing roots from those stems which fail to find a branch to support them and trail along the ground.

The fragrant Jasmine (*J. officinale*) although classed by most writers as a natural twiner, sometimes flops and needs tying. This usually happens when it is given a bulky object to twine round; it needs a slender pole or, better still, trellis-work, or the twiggy branches of a tree.

Its relative, the winter Jasmine (*J. nudiflorum*), is not a twiner but pushes its long, whip-like stems upward and over the twigs of shrubs and trees surrounding it and may reach a height of 20 feet. (In woodland where Barberries and Hawthorn grow close together, I have seen it 15 feet tall and full of flower.) The Hop (*Humulus lupulus*) is a native twiner and may be seen cultivated in Kent, its stems twisting round strings or other vertical supports.

These plants when deprived of any support mostly creep along the ground and some, like the Japanese Honeysuckle (as I have already mentioned) and the winter Jasmine, form roots on the surface (though the latter becomes quite shrubby if left untended and will in time make a pleasantly untidy hedge).

Most interesting is the movement of twiners in search of their support. The lowest portion of the stem grows erect, and the new growth which is made during the current season then bends over in search of a branch to twist round spirally. To attain the branch, the upper bending portion of the free stem revolves in a circle as though it were feeling or searching. This movement of the nutating, or bending, portion of the stem has been illustrated in several ways. The best, I think, is its comparison with a portion of a rope being twirled round one's head – a gentle circular movement of the wrist being sufficient to accomplish this. In some plants, during warm weather, the waving, revolving end makes a complete revolution in an amazingly short time. In the Bindweed (*Convolvulus arvensis*), 1 hour and 42 minutes; in the Hop, 1 hour and 57 minutes. In other twiners the motion is much slower – 24 or 48 hours being nearer the time.

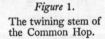

Figure 1.
The twining stem of the Common Hop.

Another interesting fact is the direction in which the free end of the stem moves. Some twiners, like the Hop, *Lonicera caprifolium* and *Polygonum convolvulus*, turn counter-clockwise (dextrorse). Others, like *Convolvulus sepium*, the Scarlet Runner and *Aristolochia macrophylla* (Dutchman's Pipe), move or twine clockwise (sinistrorse – twining or turning from right to left). Nothing can alter the direction of the movement. Heat or cold or environment has no influence on it. No scientific explanation of the cause of the different movements exists. But we know that the vital phenomena of plants, such as growth and reproduction (and perhaps the peculiar movements of some plants) depend on the constitution of their protoplasm. To this we may add

15

that a twiner continues to twist in a certain direction according to an innate tendency inherited from generation to generation.

Most twiners support themselves naturally and are therefore easy to grow. But the vigorous ones need watching to prevent them from reaching valuable shrubs and smothering them. Usually the thick trunks of trees are safe, for they are less adapted to the purpose; it is the slender-stemmed plants that a twiner grasps most easily. In fact, thread-like supports such as covered wire are ideal. Old, useless trees, however, may be used, the twining shoots being twisted round the branches and held in place by string or cord. Unfortunately this entails a lot of work. The long shoots of the evergreen Honeysuckle *Lonicera japonica* need tying very firmly. The plant twists readily enough round the thin, twiggy branches of *Buddleia davidii* (my shrub is in danger of being strangled by it).

Other climbers have other means of supporting themselves. There are those with tendrils (different types are found in different plants); those with aerial roots; those with spines or

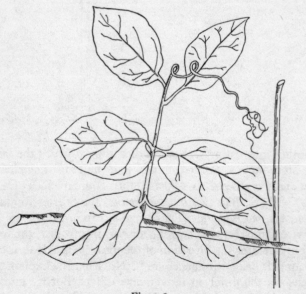

Figure 2.

Leaf of *Cobaea scandens* is composed of 3 pairs of leaflets, the end of the leaf-stalk terminating in a branched-tendril.

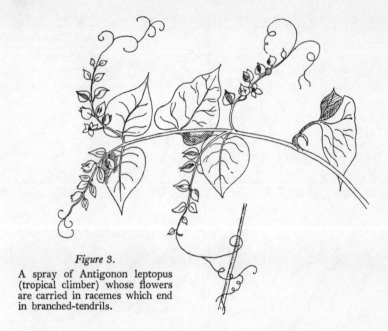

Figure 3.

A spray of Antigonon leptopus (tropical climber) whose flowers are carried in racemes which end in branched-tendrils.

prickles on their stems and sometimes on their leaves; and the spreading, shrubby plants, like *Cotoneaster horizontalis*, which push their way up walls or other flat surfaces.

Tendril-plants on the whole need little assistance. Objects unsuitable for twiners (a jagged, vertical rock, for example) can be climbed by some of them. Not normally, of course, by Clematis, which have leaf-stalk tendrils, or the common Smilax, with stipular tendrils (those that shoot out from the base of the leaf stems); but the Virginia Creeper, whose tendrils are provided with discs which adhere easily to surfaces, is capable of ascending rocks and walls and indeed smooth surfaces like glass, iron or planed wood.

In *Cobaea scandens*, a tender climber from Mexico, the four-branched tendrils come from the ends of the leaves, which are made up of three pairs of leaflets. These leaf- or midrib-tendrils are charming in appearance, arising like a delicate, silken spring. The points fasten into any object, even into a person's skin.

Antigonon leptopus is a tropical climber whose flowers are

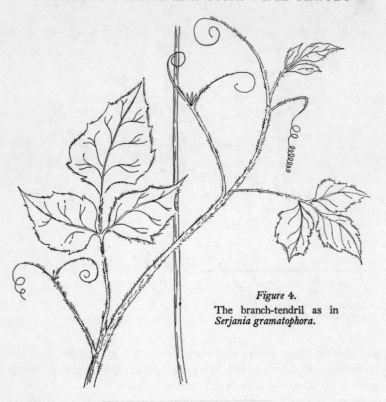

Figure 4.
The branch-tendril as in
Serjania gramatophora.

carried in racemes which end in branching tendrils; and by these
the plant ascends shrubs and trees.

Two other types of tendrils are the branch-tendril such as
occurs in the tropical climber *Serjania gramatophora*: it shoots
out from below the leaf-stalk; and the simple or undivided tendril, which is comparatively rare; our common Bryony gives us
an example of this type. The different actions or movements of
the various kinds of tendrils are discussed under the genus,
when the species, hybrids, etc., listed are described (see under
Bignonia, Clematis, Passiflora, Vitis, etc.).

Our next class of climbers consists of those with aerial roots.
Ivy is a good example. It climbs walls, rocks, trees and probably anything against which it is planted. The roots, by which
it ascends, sprout from the side of the stem turned away from
the light as do the tendrils of certain climbers – *Doxantha*

(*Bignonia*) *capreolata*, for example. They are not absorbent, the plant dying when the stem is severed at the base. Occasionally, however, when the aerial roots come across soil, say, in the crevice of some horizontal object where it is not likely to be washed away (it may be found in the crevices along the top of an old wall), these aerial roots function too as absorbent roots and take up sufficient nutrition to keep the plant alive even when the main stem has been severed.

Climbers equipped with spines, such as the Rose species (Rosa) and the Brambles (*Rubus*), send out long shoots and weave into the thickets in which they grow. Some have spines or bristles on both stems and leaves and in time grow into an inextricable tangle.

The last type we might call the lattice-stemmed plants or climbers, the young growths interlacing and pushing themselves upwards against a wall or some other flat surface. *Cotoneaster horizontalis*, which has no climbing organs, is usually quoted as an example. It neither needs training nor supporting but will grow erect slowly up the side of a house and ultimately reach a height of 5 feet or more. Planted in the open garden, it makes a creeping mass of interlacing stems, a flattish shrub most suitable for edging a border or for planting in a rockery.

Viburnum fragrans, already referred to as a wall plant, is not a shrub whose stems naturally grow lattice-like. They need training and supporting either by nailing or by tying in order to get them to grow flat against a wall. *Forsythia suspensa*, with its long, arching stems, needs training similarly if it is to cover a wall.

[4]

THE history of ornamental climbers does not go back so far as that of the economic ones like the Grape and the Hop. The latter is a native as is the Blackberry (*Rubus laciniatus*) and both are much valued by us, the first for its green cones or catkins used in the brewing of beer, and the other for its fruit. Neither would be wanted in a garden. (I have, however, seen the Hop growing up wire-netting and making an attractive screen.)

But the Grape (*Vitis vinifera*) is quite ornamental in October and November with its clusters of blue-black berries and its tinted leaves. It is said to be a native of the Caucasus and was probably introduced into Britain via Italy by the Romans. It is known to have been cultivated in our southern counties at that time and is mentioned in some of the manuscripts of the Middle Ages: "In every felde rype is corne; the grapes hongen on the vyne. . . ." (Laud MS. fourteenth century.) It is still cultivated out of doors in the warmest districts, the fruit producing a palatable wine. (I have this on good authority: I have not tasted it myself.)

The Hop is said to have been introduced into the South of England from Flanders about 1520, but it is mentioned much earlier than that; reference is made to it in a Latin work dated 1440: "Hoppe, sede for beyre. . . ."

While on the subject of economic climbers, we must not forget the truly decorative Scarlet Runner (*Phaseolus coccineus*), a native of America, where, in the warmer regions, it is a perennial and a magnificent sight when covered with its long racemes of scarlet flowers.

Ornamental climbers began to be cultivated in our gardens about the end of the sixteenth century. Of the few that are indigenous to Britain probably only two are planted by gardeners, viz. the Honeysuckle and more rarely *Clematis vitalba* or 'Traveller's Joy'. The latter is suitable only for the largest gardens and really decorative only when covered with its silky, fluffy seed-pods. The wild Honeysuckle is mentioned by John Gardner in *The Feast of Gardening* (1440). And Turner in his *Herbal* (1562) says: "Wodbynde or Honeysuckle windeth it self about busshes." Now and then it may have been collected from the hedges and planted in gardens: used perhaps to train over an arch or an arbour, for the arbour or "Bowre of boughs or trees" was a feature of some gardens at that time. It is a good plant to sit near, its scent being one of the most delightful of all flower scents.

I have not included our lovely Wild Rose (*Rosa canina*) among the ornamental native climbers; nor of course the striking, scarlet-berrying twiner, the Black Bryony (*Tamus communis*), whose berries are poisonous and have been known to kill; and the Wild Rose is best left in the hedges, for it cannot

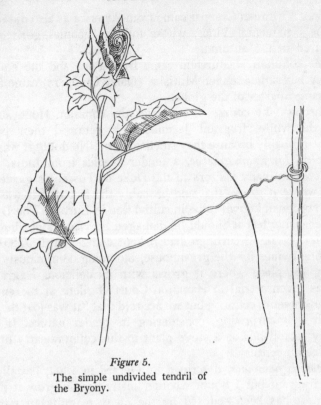

Figure 5.
The simple undivided tendril of
the Bryony.

vie with the roses that have come from the East and have
been cultivated by us from time immemorial.

The common, white Jasmine and some of the Clematis
species from southern Europe were described by botanists and
writers about the middle of the sixteenth century. The first is
mentioned by Turner in his *Names of Herbes* (1584); and
Clematis viticella and a double form appear in Gerard's *Herbal*
(1597): "They grow in my garden at Holborn and flourish
exceedingly." *Clematis flammula* was another species from
southern Europe which was in cultivation then. It is delightfully
fragrant, like the white Jasmine; but neither is particularly
showy.

The Wistaria (*W. sinensis*) was not introduced till the beginning of the nineteenth century; and about that time many of
our loveliest and most treasured climbers began to arrive. The

brilliant Virginian Creeper came from America as also did some of the ornamental Vines, whose foliage becomes gorgeously coloured in the autumn.

The common Nasturtium came from Peru and the equally showy but rather tender Mutisias (Daisy Creepers) came from the same quarter of the globe.

Through the course of centuries the common Honeysuckle and the white, fragrant Jasmine have retained their popularity, probably because they smell so good. No doubt it was the scent of *Jasminum sambac*, a tender species from India, that attracted so many visitors to the Duke of Tuscany's garden at Pisa where it grew: that and probably the fact that it was the only specimen known to be in cultivation in Europe. The Duke, apprehensive lest it should be damaged by visitors picking the flowers or taking cuttings, had it kept under guard. *J. sambac* is a fine twiner for the greenhouse, blooming continuously and filling the place where it grows with its delicious fragrance. It was given a trial in Hampton Court Gardens at the end of the seventeenth century, but we are told that "it was lost there", which isn't surprising, considering its tender nature. It was finally established as a stove plant in this country early in the eighteenth century.

Clematis flammula, described by Gerard in 1597, is delightfully fragrant but I doubt whether many people grow it nowadays. It has been eclipsed by the many magnificent garden forms, which owe their origin to some of the Asiatic species (*C. lanuginosa* from China; and *C. patens* from Japan, are two) introduced during the middle of the nineteenth century. The popular *C.* × *Jackmanii* was one of the first, raised about 1860, a striking velvety purple flower beloved by so many gardeners. Not many would hesitate if they had to choose between this hybrid and one of the small-flowered species.

Undoubtedly the garden forms of the Clematis are the most popular of all the climbers we grow. The first section of the following chapter is devoted to them and the best-known species.

C.C. florida, lanuginosa, patens (no longer in cultivation) are included because they are the types from which many of our large-flowered garden varieties are derived.

CHAPTER ONE

Climbers for the Garden

(*Including the most popular kinds*)

[1]

CLEMATIS is derived from a Greek word which was used to describe some kind of climbing or trailing plant; and in Latin, *Clematis* is thought to have been the Periwinkle (*Vinca minor*). The word was used by Pliny (A.D. 23–79) in his Natural History (*Historiae Naturalis*). The pronunciation with the accent on the first syllable is correct but one often hears *Cle-maytis*.

There are well over 200 species, the plants being widely distributed over the temperate regions of both hemispheres. They occur chiefly, however, in the northern regions, several species being native to Europe. Only one, *C. vitalba*, is indigenous to this country. (The specific epithet is a contraction of *vitis*: vine; and *alba*: white.) It is the Traveller's Joy or Old Man's Beard, the latter name being suggested no doubt by the white silky hairs of the seeds. The plant is not suitable for the average garden; it is far too rampant and will eventually strangle shrubs and trees on which it grows.

Clematis belong to the Buttercup family (*Ranunculaceae*) but unlike that flower have no true petals. The spreading petal-like organs – often showy and beautifully coloured – are actually sepals: usually four, but up to eight in number.

Botanists have divided the genus into 2 groups, viz. (1) *Atragene*, in which one or more rows of abortive stamens or enlarged petals (petaloid staminodes) come between the sepals and the stamens. (*C. alpina* is a well-known species of this type.) (2) *Viorna*, in which the sepals form a bell- or urn-shaped flower, the sepals being connivent or narrowing toward the points. (*C. texensis* has this type of flower; see also *C. tangutica*.)

Clematis flowers vary enormously in size and shape. In the most popular section, which contains the garden varieties, they are large, open blooms, some 8 or more inches across. In the Vitalba section they are small and come in panicles as in *C. flammula*.

The former are the kinds most widely planted in our gardens. They are derived from various species and from the hybrid *C. × Jackmanii* and are consequently listed under types known as Florida, Jackmanii, Lanuginosa, Patens, Viticella. These are the most important. It is not possible to label them strictly, for many are of mixed parentage. The hybrid *C. × Jackmanii*, for instance, has *lanuginosa* blood in it and is itself the type plant of the Jackmanii Group.

C. florida (full of flowers). A native of China and collected near Ichang, Hupeh, by the botanist Henry. The original plant introduced by Thunberg in 1776 from Japan was probably a cultivated form. The species is a deciduous or partly evergreen climber with strong stems and eventually attains a height of about 12 feet. Each flower is carried singly on a stalk 3 or 4 inches long which, about half-way up, has two leaf-like bracts. The flowers, about 4 inches wide, are made up of 4 to 6 spreading, white or cream oval sepals marked with a greenish band down the back. In the centre is a conspicuous ring of dark purple stamens. The leaves (3 to 5 inches long) are divided into 3 segments, each of which consists of 3 leaflets. It is an attractive climber, blooming in June and July. The variety *C. florida* var. *sieboldii*, with a centre packed with purple stamens, is a form sometimes grown in our gardens. I have not been able to obtain a specimen from any nursery; and I doubt whether the species itself is now in cultivation. It is one of the parents of some very lovely large-flowered garden Clematis. The following are classed under the Florida Group. They can be got from most shrub nurseries and are some of the choicest.

'Belle of Woking,' with pale silvery-mauve flowers, double, and blooming in May and June.

'Countess of Lovelace' is of a charming bluish-lilac colour; the flower, double, rosette-shaped. May and June.

'Duchess of Edinburgh.' Another double type. Pure white and fragrant.

'Lucie Lemoine' is also white but not fragrant. A double type with yellow anthers and blooming in July.

'Proteus.' Large, mauve-pink flowers usually at their best in June. Mr. G. R. Jackman in a lecture on Clematis given at Vincent Square in July, 1958, singled it out for special mention. "For anyone who wants a clematis that is 'different', I can recommend 'Proteus'. The pink flowers suffused with plum-purple are of a colour not found in any other variety. The first flowers, which open at the end of May, are double, and when it blooms again later in the summer all the second crop is single."

I have seen it blooming profusely in a cold greenhouse and it was really a glorious sight. Gardeners living in cold, northern districts state that the Florida Varieties are less hardy than many other types: those, for example, classed under Lanuginosa.

As regards pruning: this should be done after the blooming season; the flowers are carried on short, side shoots that come from the growths made during the previous season. They must be cut back to a bud at the base.

My experience with these beautifully coloured varieties is that they last longer in partial shade; in full sun the colours fade quickly.

C. × *Jackmanii* is nominally the head of our next group. It has retained its enormous popularity over the years despite the many lovelier varieties that have appeared on the market.

The first plants were raised at the nurseries of Messrs. Jackman of Woking and flowered there in 1862. They were named in honour of the raisers. The parentage is given as *C. lanuginosa* × *C.* × *Hendersonii*, though this has been disputed.

C × *Jackmanii* grows about as tall as *C. florida* and is completely hardy, doing well in most gardens in this country. The leaves are 3-foliolate or simple. The flowers hardly need describing: the petal-like sepals number from 4 to 6, their violet-purple being among the richest colours in our gardens.

These varieties are regarded as the most reliable of the garden Clematis; they bloom more profusely and seem to be more successful than many of the others. It is the group from which amateur gardeners usually choose their large-flowered kinds. The following are some of the best.

'Comtesse de Bouchaud' is one of the old varieties – a charming pink tinged with mauve. It blooms in July and August.

'Gypsy Queen' is another; it resembles the type plant, but the colour is darker. It was listed in most catalogues twenty years ago and incidentally cost then about 3s. (the current price of many of these Clematis is about 10s. 6d.). This variety is recommended by most specialists. It opens in late July and goes on well into August.

'Jackmanii alba.' Quoting from an early Hillier catalogue: "It bears large, double white flowers in June, and single flowers, white suffused blue, in August." It is lovely on a tree, where it will require no pruning.

'Jackmanii rubra' is a reddish-purple shade; a free flowerer. July and August.

'Jackmanii superba.' Magnificent on a tree where its long shoots can hang down and show off the dark violet blooms. I think it superior to most of the purple Clematis.

'Madame Edouard André' has bright velvety-red flowers with yellow stamens. It blooms freely in July and August.

'Perle d'Azur' has light blue flowers and is a very free bloomer.

I have had some of these Clematis in bloom as late as October, and where they are climbing over large shrubs or up trees they are left untouched. In limited spaces, in small gardens, it is often necessary to cut them back. Pruning must be done in February; cut back the previous year's growth to within about 9 inches of the base. Many gardeners prefer to leave them, however, so that they get an early show of flowers.

C. lanuginosa (woolly; referring to the leaves and the flower-stalks). It is the plant from which are derived many beautiful, large-flowered garden Clematis. Like *C. florida*, it is not offered for sale by nurseries. In its habitat, Eastern China, where it was found by Robert Fortune in 1850, it grows no taller than 6 feet. The cultivated garden varieties, however, usually go up to a height of 12 feet. The species is deciduous and has leaves of a thick texture; they may be simple or composed of 3 leaf-lets. The flowers, which are white or pale lilac, have from 6 to 8 sepals, wide-spreading and overlapping. The seed-vessels have long, silky tails. (In the Clematis genus the seed or the fruit is known as an achene, which Lindley described as "any small brittle, seed-like fruit such as Linnaeus called a naked seed".)

Some of the best varieties of the Lanuginosa Group are:

'Beauty of Richmond.' Mr. Jackman describes it: "The flowers are lovely in shape, the sepals being long and with flowing curves. They are mauve, and the bar down the centre of each is the same colour but deeper."

'Beauty of Worcester.' A single and double flower; blue-violet; conspicuous white stamens. At its best usually in July.

'Blue Gem' is a lovely shade of pale sky-blue.

'Crimson King.' Rich rosy-red; stamens chocolate coloured. July and August.

'Elsa Spath' blooms profusely and is very vigorous. Its colour is a light lavender-blue; the stamens are much darker.

'Henryi.' White. An old favourite variety. An extra large flower, with long, pointed sepals. July and August.

'King Edward VII.' Puce-violet, with a crimson bar down the centre of each sepal.

'Lady Caroline Neville.' Pale mauve with a darker-coloured bar. June and July.

'Lady Northcliffe.' Deep lavender tinted with light blue, the sepals shaded purple at base. June to September.

'Marie Boissilot.' A lovely, white flower with yellow stamens. July to September.

'Mrs. Cholmondeley.' An early bloomer: May and June. A charming light blue colour. Very free.

'W. E. Gladstone.' A large flower, the lilac sepals being a lighter shade in the middle.

'William Kennett.' The sepals have a wavy edge; the colour is lavender – darker in the centre.

Most of these varieties bloom during summer and autumn. Any pruning that is necessary should be done in February or March, the flowers coming on the growths made in the spring. By leaving the plants untouched, they will bloom earlier and grow taller.

C. patens (spreading; the epithet refers to the wide-spreading sepals of the flower). This species, not in cultivation here, is common in Japanese gardens, whence it was introduced to Europe by the botanist Siebold about the middle of the last century. It is deciduous and grows about 12 feet tall. The leaves are made up of 3 or 5 leaflets; the flowers, 4 to 6 inches, are solitary and come on stems which have no bracts – this character distinguishes the species from *C. florida*, with which it is allied. The colour of the flowers of the wild plant is white. In the cultivated forms it ranges from white through mauve to deep violet-blue.

Some recommended varieties are:

'Barbara Dibley.' A deep rich violet, with deeper-coloured bars; a variety related to the well-known 'Nelly Moser', as is

'Barbara Jackman.' A shade of soft petunia, the bar on each sepal is plum-coloured, and the stamens are cream. A beautiful flower, which likes a fairly shady spot. May and June.

'Edouard Desfosse', a very large flower which I have often seen exhibited at shows. A deep violet-mauve; darker bars. May and June.

'Lady Londesborough.' A delicate mauve; the bar down each sepal is a paler colour.

'Lasursten.' Another very large flower. A deep purplish-blue; the stamens are yellow. Usually blooms in May and June but does not give a second (September) show as do some of these varieties.

'Nelly Moser' is the next most famous garden Clematis after *C.* × *Jackmanii*. It is seen in many of our gardens. The sepals are pale mauve-pink with a deep carmine bar down the middle.

'President' is often listed in catalogues as 'The President'. Deep violet flowers with a paler bar. Dark anthers. Blooms in June and again in September. It tolerates plenty of sun; most of the others, however, prefer a north or a north-west aspect.

Any pruning of these early-flowering varieties should be done after the blooming season. Apart from spreading out, and thinning out their stems which often grow tangled, I seldom touch them.

C. viticella (an old Latin name of a plant; probably a vine; but not actually known). The popular name is The Vine Bower. The species, a native of southern Europe, was grown in Britain during the sixteenth century. It is not wholly woody in this country, the stem often dying back in winter. Normally it reaches a height of 8 to 12 feet. The leaves, deciduous, are usually much divided, the leaflets being from ½ inch to 2 inches long. The flowers, which are fragrant, sometimes come in threes; the sepals, usually 4 in number, are blue, purple or rosy-red, and make a cross-shaped bloom, very attractive with its centre of yellow stamens. The species may be obtained from most shrub specialists and, with it, some of the old varieties which have long been known in our gardens. The best known are: 'albiflora', with white flowers; 'alba luxurians', white flowers, tinted mauve; 'kermesina', a striking shade of wine-red.

The Viticella Clematis include both large- and small-flowered varieties and they bloom late.

'Ernest Markham' is recommended as the best of the reds. It flowers from July to September.

'Étoile Violette' will carry thousands of blooms, when it has become well established. A deep violet flower with contrasting yellow stamens. A comparatively small flower – about 4 inches across.

'Huldine' blooms late, usually in September and October; it has pearly-white flowers, their translucent quality showing up the mauve bar down the centre beautifully when the sun catches them.

'Lady Betty Balfour,' with deep velvety-purple flowers, is another late bloomer. I have seen it full of flower in mid-October.

'Ville de Lyon' is an old variety with bright, carmine-red sepals which are a much deeper shade round the edge.

Pruning, if any, should be done early; the dead wood is cut back to within about 9 inches of the base. The new growth that shoots out will carry the season's flowers.

C. viticella is best raised from cuttings: seed is not always reliable.

All these Clematis need a deep rich loam and they like lime. On thin soils, calcareous types included, they are a failure. Heavy clay is excellent if it is broken up and mixed with weathered ashes and leafmould.

Dig the soil deeply and add plenty of old, well-rotted cow

manure. The best time for planting is September and October, the preparation of the soil being done in the spring. The following March cut them back drastically to a bud within 6 inches of the base. This initial treatment of all types of Clematis encourages strong, healthy growth. Similarly, pinching out the tips of too vigorous shoots encourages them to branch and flower, but it should not be done later than June.

People like to see many of the large-flowered Clematis growing up a wall. They will not, of course, ascend brickwork without something suitable for their leaf-tendrils to cling to. Trellis-work set close to the wall, or wires stretched horizontally at intervals of 12 inches up the wall, are the best supports.

Of the many different Clematis species that have come to us from various parts of the world, I have seen not more than a dozen growing in our gardens. All of these – and others – can be obtained from many of our nurseries.

C. alpina (growing in alpine places). A native of Central and Southern Europe and North-east Asia, where at high altitudes it blooms in May. With us it is often at its best in April and is thus one of the first of the Clematis to open. It is a charming climber, seldom more than 6 feet tall and has been seen by many visitors to the Alps, who have found it clambering over bushes and covered with nodding, bluish flowers.

The leaves are deciduous, the largest 6 inches long, each leaf composed of 9 leaflets which are coarsely-toothed. The flowers have four sepals, blue or tinged with violet; between the centre of the stamens and the sepals is a ring of spoon-shaped, petal-like organs (found, too, in *C. macropetala* and in *C. verticillaris*); they are not conspicuous but distinguish these species from the others. The flowers are comparatively small, but a plant in full flush in April is a lovely sight.

The variety *C. alpina* var. *sibirica* is better known; it is more robust and has yellowish-white sepals forming a nodding, bell-shaped flower. 'Columbine' is a good single form; and *C. alpina sibirica* 'White Moth' has double flowers. The plants like a cool, shady place and are disappointing in full sun; a fairly rich loam that doesn't dry out is required.

Little pruning is necessary: thinning out of the old growths is sufficient; this should be done in winter. Propagation is by seeds or by cuttings placed in a frame in August.

(Synonyms are *Atragene alpina* and *Atragene sibirica*.) The species and its varieties are obtainable from most shrub specialists.

C. armandii (Armand's Clematis).[1] A Chinese species often described as "a noble evergreen requiring a sunny sheltered wall". It is a valuable climber, for we haven't many evergreen kinds. As it is on the tender side, it needs a wall. It is by no means popular: its slight tenderness deters many of us from growing it. But Clematis-lovers invariably include it in their collections and if they haven't a warm wall, grow it against the south side of the house. Which is an ideal place for it. It may reach a height of 20 feet in time and is lovely when its branching stems are covered with flowers. These, white, fragrant and 2 inches wide, come in axillary clusters about the end of April or early in May. The large, glossy evergreen leaves are made up of 3 leaflets and are attractive even when the plant is not in bloom. Their colour and their leathery texture make them an excellent foil to the white flowers.

This climber may not need pruning for some years. It is best left to grow as big as we want it and then to prune it judiciously after it has finished flowering. Weak shoots and dead wood should be cut out; drastic pruning may be done in February, though consequently a season's flowers will be sacrificed.

Some plants of this species that I have come across in gardens have not been particularly good. I recommend 'Snowdrift', a variety with pure white flowers, and 'Apple Blossom', whose flowers are tinted pink in the bud; the leaves are a bronzy-green.

In warm countries the Armandii Clematis are often grown on trees and left untouched. On a wall, of course, they will need some sort of support.

The species is native to Central and Western China. Wilson introduced it for Messrs. Veitch in 1900.

C. chrysocoma (with a tuft of golden hairs: the shoots, leaves and flower-stalks are all covered with a dense golden-yellow down). The popular name is the Hairy Clematis.

---

[1] A fine specimen is trained on a wall at the Savill Gardens, Windsor. (The stems growing along the top were covered with flowers on April 20th, 1959.) The main, woody stems are bare for some 6 feet up from the base.

On the whole this species from China is easier to grow than the preceding, but it is not very well known. Ernest Markham in his book on Clematis says: "I know of no more lovely Clematis than this, nor any more easily grown." Marchant's catalogue describes it as "not quite hardy". Everybody who grows it praises it for its lovely pinkish-white flowers, which resemble those of *C. montana*. *C. chrysocoma* carries its flowers on stalks about 3 inches in length, which spring from the joints of the previous year's growth. It is a favourite Clematis for cutting; few of the others are suitable for this purpose. The leaves are 3-foliolate, the leaflets being from 1 to 2 inches long and covered with shaggy yellow down.

This charming Clematis, which will reach a height of 12 feet or more (though in the open garden it often doesn't grow tall) blooms twice: first in June and then again in October. It is usually classed with the Montana type and is regarded as being less rampant than *C. montana* itself. But I have seen the former grow as tall, covering a tree with thousands of its exquisite pink and white flowers. It is impossible then to prune it; on a wall this is easily done; the faded flowers should be clipped over and the dead wood and weak growths cut out.

The habitat of the species is Yunnan, China, where it was first discovered growing on mountain slopes at altitudes of 7,000–9,000 feet by the Abbé Delavay in 1884. It has not proved completely hardy at Kew. The first specimen arrived there via France, introduced in 1910 by Mr. Maurice Vilmorin. In the warm south it begins blooming in early May and continues till the autumn. Most shrub nurseries stock it.

C. flammula. (The specific epithet is a Latin word meaning a little flame or banner.) L. H. Bailey in the *Manual of Cultivated Plants* states, "*a little flame*, an ante-Linnaean application to this plant." The popular name is the Fragrant Virgin's Bower.

This deciduous species, a native of southern Europe, was introduced from France into England toward the end of the sixteenth century; but it has never been widely grown. It should be on account of its mass of small white flowers which are deliciously fragrant and, moreover, come in August when there is a dearth of flowers in our gardens. The plant is slender and goes up to a height of 12 or 15 feet, a mature specimen making a top-heavy-looking tangle, which is always lovely to look at.

The lower parts of the stems are bare. I prefer not to prune it, and leave it like this for some years, then to cut a few of the old stems back drastically and the remainder the following year. Spring is the best time for the work.

The individual flowers, from ¾ inch to 1 inch wide, are carried in loose panicles about 12 inches long. The scent has been compared to that of almonds and is perceptible from a good distance. The leaves vary much in size and shape; they are often composed of 3 or 5 leaflets, these being usually 3-foliolate.

C. flammula is completely hardy and is variously used; I have seen it on walls, trellis-work, arches and on bushes and trees. It looks best on the trees, which is how it grows in the wild.

An attractive hybrid between the species and *C. viticella* is *C. × violacea rubro-marginata*, which blooms at the same time as *C. flammula* and has fragrant white flowers margined with rose-pink.

Both plants are offered for sale by most shrub nurseries.

C. × Jouiniana (named in honour of Mr. E. Jouin of the Simon-Louis nurseries at Metz).

The parentage of this exquisite hybrid is the herbaceous *C. heracleifolia Davidiana × C. vitalba*, our native Clematis. *C. × Jouiniana* makes an enormous amount of growth in a season (12 feet or more) and blooms simultaneously with *C. flammula*. I have seen both growing together on trees and shrubs. In one garden the two practically covered an old apple-tree, an inferior variety, however, not valued for its fruit.

The flowers of the hybrid are small, coming in corymbs, 4 to 6 inches long, from the leaf-axils and forming compound panicles several feet in length. Each flower is made up of 4 strap-shaped sepals, pointed, and ¾ inch long; the colour is yellowish-white at first and then it becomes tinged with lilac. The flowers are slightly fragrant.

The leaves, deciduous and intermediate between those of the parents, are composed of 3 or 5 leaflets.

Several seedling forms of *C. × Jouiniana*, inheriting the characteristics of the herbaceous parent, are in cultivation: 'heracleifolia Côte d'Azur' is the best known; the small star-shaped flowers are azure-blue, the leaves a pleasant glossy green. A pretty, little climber for the front of a border, where there is a low bush for it to trail over.

The *Jouiniana* Clematis are best propagated by cuttings under glass. Apart from cutting out dead wood and weak shoots, little pruning is necessary. It is usually done in late winter.

C. macropetala (with large petals). Its popular name is the Downy Clematis; the different parts of the flowers are covered with down. The plant was at one time known as *Atragene macropetala*; *Atragene*, as already stated, is now that section of the genus in which the flowers have a ring of staminodes between the sepals and the stamens.

The flower has been described as having a 'bunched-up' appearance, the centre being packed with numerous petal-like segments. There are 4 sepals about 2 inches long and ⅓ inch wide, blue or violet-blue in colour. It is an uncommonly beautiful flower, usually nodding or carried in a semi-horizontal position.

This deciduous climber, a native of Kansu, China, and of Siberia, reaches a height of about 8 feet and is particularly attractive draping a low wall. Although it was known to botanists more than 200 years ago (d'Incarville discovered it north of Peking in 1742) it was not introduced into Britain till 1912. It first flowered at Kew in 1920 and has since become fairly widely grown. The species and the varieties derived from it are obtainable from most nurseries. I think the loveliest is *C. macropetala* var. Markhamii raised by Ernest Markham; its flowers are a clear pink. Another charming form is 'Maidwell Hall', whose flowers are intermediate between Oxford and Cambridge blue.

Pruning should be done immediately the flowers have faded. Mr. Markham in his book *Clematis* says, "The weak shoots should be removed, and the remainder spread out at 8 inches apart, shortening them to sound wood."

Propagation is usually by layering or by cuttings.

C. montana (growing in mountainous places). Its popular name is The Great Indian Clematis. It comes from the Himalayas where it reaches a height of 30 feet or more, its long stems covered with pure white open flowers.

The soft-pink *C. montana* var. *rubens* is a natural form widely distributed in Western China, where the white is not found. Both are beautiful and very common in our gardens. Next to

C. × *Jackmanii* they are, I imagine, the most popular of the Clematis we grow.

Although the variety sold by nurseries (called 'grandiflora') has larger flowers and is preferred by many gardeners, it is the smaller-flowered plant that we see in most gardens. It is vigorous, hardy and easily accommodated. Sun or shade suits it; it is lovely on a tree or on a wall or hanging from horizontal supports, say, along a veranda, where its long growths can stream down and show off the white anemone-like flowers to perfection. It is a simple flower, with 4 spreading, pure white sepals and a centre of yellow stamens. It measures 2 inches across and comes singly on a longish stem, but as several spring from the axils of the leaves the flowers seem to be in clusters. The leaves have 3 leaflets, from about 2 to 4 inches long, and are pointed and toothed.

In the variety *rubens* they are similarly shaped but purplish in colour and more downy. This purplish tinge to the foliage harmonizes beautifully with the soft pink flowers. These bloom a little later than those of the type: usually about the beginning of May.[1] The plant is a profuse bloomer, never failing to carry thousands of pink blossoms and is even hardier than the other. Bean says of it, "This variety is probably the most beautiful and useful climber distributed in the twentieth century." It was collected for Messrs. Veitch by Wilson in China in 1900, almost 70 years after the white type was introduced from India by Lady Amherst.

There is another form from China called var. *Wilsonii*, with white, fragrant flowers opening in July and August.

Other forms set out by nurseries are var. *undulata*, which has mauvish-white flowers, and 'Elizabeth', with large soft-pink flowers. (L. H. Bailey give the parentage of the former as *C. montana* × *C. gracilifolia*.)

I prefer to propagate the Montana Clematis by cuttings or by layers and to prune them after the leaves have fallen, say, in December when all the stems and the various shoots are fully exposed.

C. spooneri (Spooner's Clematis). Marchant describes it as

---

[1] Two lovely old plants grow on a wall of the quadrangle of All Souls, Oxford. Their thick woody stems at the base are about 2 inches in diameter. The flowers are at their best usually during the first week in May.

"A better climber, for general planting, than the beautiful *C. chrysocoma*". It is classed with the Montana type and blooms about the same time as *C. montana*.[1] It is allied with the Chinese *C. chrysocoma* and has often been described as *C. chrysocoma sericea* (silky). The leaves are clothed with a yellowish, silky down.

This deciduous climber attains a height of 20 feet and is a strong, vigorous plant; like the hybrid *C.* × *Jouiniana* described above, it makes a long stem in a single season. The species, native to Western China, was introduced by Wilson in 1909.

There is a very charming pink form called *C. spooneri* var. *rosea* with flowers of a deep apple-blossom pink. So far, I have not been able to get it anywhere; but the white type plant is obtainable from most nurseries.

C. tangutica (sometimes referred to as the Tangut Clematis. Tangut was formerly a North Tibetan kingdom in North-west China in the regions of Ningsia and Nansu). The popular name is the Golden Clematis.

This deciduous species is famed for its yellow flowers, which are the finest of the three yellow-flowered Clematis that we grow in our gardens. They are of a rich golden-yellow shade, urn-shaped and nodding, and come on stems 3 to 6 inches long. The silky, grey seed-heads, often 6 inches across (like miniature mops) make the plant one of the most decorative and arresting in the autumn garden. Often there is a good show of late flowers and seeds together. The leaves are greyish-green and raggedly-toothed.

Although the plant is often described as a vigorous climber, it does not go above 10 feet in height and is excellent for training on a low wall – up one side and down the other. Or it may be grown on a bush like *Buddleia davidii*, whose long panicles of mauve flowers are at their best when the silky seed-heads of the Clematis begin to form.

The variety, *C. tangutica obtusiuscula* (somewhat blunt) may be distinguished by its smaller leaves, its more woolly appear-

---

[1] E. H. M. Cox in *Farrer's Last Journey* mentions *C. spooneri*. "Botanists tell you of the close resemblance of *C. spooneri* to *C. montana*. That may be so in dried specimens, but is certainly not the case when alive. *C. spooneri* is a gorgeous plant without a single blemish that we could discover." The flowers, beautifully illustrated in a photograph, are wide-opened, with four sepals, waved and pointed and deeply marked with veining.

ance, and by the sepals which are blunt or rounder than those of the type plant's: these are long and pointed. It is perhaps not so decorative as the type; but some nurseries offer it instead of the other. Hillier's listed it in their 1955–56 catalogue where it was priced at 7s. 6d.

C. tangutica is a native of China and Mongolia and was introduced to Kew from St. Petersburg in 1898. The variety comes from West Szechwan, China, where it flourishes luxuriantly at altitudes of 8,000 to 10,000 feet; Wilson introduced it in 1908.

Little pruning is necessary for either; February is the best month for any that has to be done. Propagation is by cuttings or by layering.

C. texensis a (native of Texas; it was discovered there in 1850 and introduced in 1868). It has, like the preceding species, urn-shaped, nodding flowers, their colour, however, being scarlet or carmine. No doubt many a gardener has been surprised to learn that the two described above and this species were Clematis. For their flowers are the antithesis of the normal open Clematis flower.

In this country the plant does not grow taller than 5 or 6 feet and is herbaceous in character, the stems dying back to ground level during the winter.

It will need a warm, sheltered wall in most districts and where it grows well, it is enchanting with its small scarlet, nodding flowers and contrasting glaucous green leaves. There is a good specimen at Kew Botanic Gardens, trained against the foot of a south wall.

In its native habitat, it is vigorous and woody and gives a brilliant show in midsummer. Propagation is usually by cuttings under glass; and because of its tender nature, it is wise to take a few every year.

Better known than the species are the garden varieties derived from it, though they are not by any means so popular as the varieties of Lanuginosa, Patens, etc., described at the beginning of the chapter. There are about half a dozen obtainable; their flowers are larger than those of the type.

'Admiration' has salmon-pink flowers edged with mauve.

'Countess of Onslow' is a bright purple flower with a red band down each sepal.

'Duchess of Albany.' Bright rosy-pink flowers.

'Duchess of York.' The flowers are a deep pink fading towards the margins of the sepals; the effect is pinkish-white.

'Grace Darling' has a lovely rose-carmine flower.

'Gravetye Beauty.' A more open flower than most of the other varieties. Deep glowing red.

'Sir Trevor Lawrence' has flowers of a striking shade of carmine-red.

These garden forms as a rule are more vigorous than the species itself. They are pruned in spring by cutting them back to a bud at the base of the stems. The Texensis garden Clematis deserve to be more widely grown: they need perhaps a little more care and attention than the others.

In the preceding pages I have described about a dozen different species; and these, together with the many different garden varieties, will provide a show of flowers successively from April to October. Other species, which are included in the following chapter on rarer climbers, would extend the flowering season and give us practically a year of Clematis flowers: *C. calycina*, for example, blooms in January as does *C. cirrhosa*. With a wide selection of species and varieties it would be possible to have a Clematis Garden. They give us a good range of colours – almost every shade except orange – and variety in shape and form of flowers and foliage, and fragrance. Diversity in habit of growth can be obtained if we train them in various ways: over tree-stumps so that the plants become bush-like; they may be spread out on walls or allowed to clamber like vines up trees, or trained to give a cascade effect over wire structures (similar to those used for Weeping or Rambler Roses). And some of the large-flowered Garden Clematis are planted away from any supports, in beds of their own and allowed to form round, flattish masses of brilliant colour – they are grown in this way at Kew. The only disadvantage here, is that during wet weather, the flowers being so near the soil become spattered with mud. If, however, the bed is cut out on a lawn, there is less possibility of their being spoiled.

In a small garden there may be, possibly, some difficulty in accommodating them; for the few shrubs and trees that are grown will undoubtedly be all valuable ones – fruiting or flowering kinds. But a single species or one of the large-flowered varieties may be trained up wires or slender, wooden supports fixed against the wall of the house; the semi-shady side is best. The supports must be thin, slender, wire-like, because Clematis are tendril-climbers or, more specifically, leaf-stalk tendril-climbers. (See Fig. 6.) They cannot grasp thick branches.

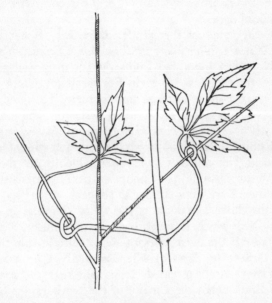

Figure 6.
The leaf-stalk tendril of the Clematis.

When the leaf-stalks make contact with a twig, they begin to curve round it like a ring. This movement is caused by the stimulus the stalks get, and they always curve towards the side which has been touched or pressed by the twig.

Finally, Clematis of all types like shade round their roots and a cool root-run. This is easily provided by a boulder sunk well down into the soil on the sunny side of the plants. Many gardeners prefer to grow a dwarf evergreen shrub against them, which is almost as good.

[2]

JASMINE, by which most people mean the twiner with white, fragrant flowers, was grown in our gardens before any of the Clematis; it was probably the first of the decorative climbers to be introduced here.

The Latin name of the genus, *Jasminum*, comes from the Persian, *Yasmin*. The plant is *Jasminum officinale*, a native of Persia, Northern India and China; and it may well have been brought from the East by early European travellers (it bears good crops of berries in those hot countries but does not fruit regularly with us). It is often called *Jessamine*, the name being used mostly for this species. Gerard in his *Herbal* says, "The yellow Jasmine differeth not from the common white Gesmine." (Jessamine.) The yellow (*J. fruticans*, which is not the popular yellow Winter Jasmine) is by no means as fragrant as the white; but the flowers are very similar in shape.

From the flowers of some of the white Jasmines an essential oil is distilled which is much used in perfumery. The tender *J. grandiflora* is the most fragrant and is cultivated in the 'scent' fields of Grasse (S. France) where annually 1,720,000 pounds of the flowers are harvested. It is said that the scent is so powerful that on hot days many of the workers are overcome by it and faint.

In the seventeenth century Jessamine or Jasmine ointment and cosmetics were in common use: people had their pots of "double refined Jesminy"; and barbers used to "Jecimy the hair", which was "to put Jecimy on the palms of the hands and rub it into the hair".

The genus comprises some 200 species which come from tropical, temperate and sub-tropical regions. Not more than a dozen kinds, however, are suitable for cultivation in this country. And we seldom see more than six: the two: *J. officinale* and *J. nudiflorum* are grown everywhere; but the hardy *J. beesianum* is rare and several of the others are too tender for outside. There are about 7 climbing or semi-climbing sorts listed in catalogues; and occasionally one or two of shrubby habit are included.

Jasmines are easy to grow, requiring ordinary well-drained loam and plenty of sun. But to get the best show of flowers from the yellow winter bloomer, *J. nudiflorum*, it must be planted against a north wall; the plant will need support; either trellis, or wires, since it is not a natural twiner like the fragrant, summer *J. officinale*, which will twist round slender stems or sticks.

Propagation of the plants is mostly by layers or by cuttings. The yellow winter Jasmine has the useful habit of rooting its long stems in the soil when they are allowed to trail instead of being supported.

Because there are so few Jasmines in cultivation here, I have included the uncommon ones with the popular and, describing them in alphabetical order, begin with the rarely seen *J. beesianum* (named for the firm of Bees, Ltd., for whom it was collected in 1906 by Forrest; it was subsequently introduced by that firm).

This is the only Jasmine that has red or carmine-coloured flowers. As they are fragrant too, one would imagine that the plant would be very popular. It is a completely hardy climber about 10 feet high, but unfortunately the flowers do not come very freely – at least in this country. They are small and rather hidden by the dark green oval-shaped leaves. The species' great attraction, I think, is the many hanging clusters of glossy, black berries which are so conspicuous on the leafless stems and last well into the winter.

It is a native of Szechwan and Yunnan, where it is sometimes found as an erect shrub up to 5 feet tall and sometimes as a climber.

Forrest collected all his specimens in the Lichiang Range, at altitudes of from 8,000 to 10,000 feet, most of them shrub-like plants growing in dry, open places. Wilson and Schneider also collected it in the same district in 1914, the latter stating that the species was a climber which was nearly always found trailing over hedges. Most shrub specialists stock it. Hillier's describes it as "a slender branched, somewhat scandent shrub attaining about 8 feet. Significant on account of the crimson colour of its rather small flowers."

J. floridum (flowery). It is mostly grown against a wall in this country and then goes up to a good height. It is not hardy around London and needs a warm wall such as it gets at Kew Botanic Gardens. In the south it attains a height of 8 feet or so and is pretty in late summer with its long rambling stems covered with yellow flowers. These are small and come in terminal clusters. The leaves, sometimes evergreen, are usually 3-foliolate, the leaflets narrow and measuring about 1 inch long. The species is a native of China and is widely cultivated there and in Japan; in these countries it blooms more freely than it does with us. Henry found it in Central China. The plant was introduced into Britain by the Earl of Ilchester about 1850. It is easily propagated by layers. It seems to be rare nowadays. I came across it in an old catalogue of Hillier's, where it was described as "a rare, semi-evergreen, Chinese shrub, related to *J. revolutum*. Flowers yellow in terminal cymes."

J. fruticans (shrubby Jasmine). The berries are black in the autumn, about $\frac{1}{4}$ inch wide and attractive when they are produced in quantity. The species was grown here in the sixteenth century and was mentioned by Gerard in his *Herbal* (1597). It comes from the Mediterranean region where it makes a fine shrubby plant, 5 or 6 feet high in the open, and is charming in June with its small bright yellow flowers, very similar in shape to those of the white *Jessamine* but lacking their fragrance. It has become something of a rarity now. No doubt it has been ousted by the more popular *J. nudiflorum* (the Winter Jasmine) with larger, bright yellow flowers. *J. fruticans* is semi-evergreen, or evergreen on a warm wall, where its stems will reach a height of 12 feet. And when in full bloom, the flowers show up well against the deep green foliage. The narrow leaflets, mostly in threes, average $\frac{1}{2}$ inch in length. In *The Botanical Magazine* (1799) the plant is described as the Yellow Jasmine (the popular yellow winter bloomer was not introduced till 1844) and as being "often planted against walls, pales, etc., as the branches are weak and slender and will grow to be 12 feet high if they are supported".

We occasionally see it as a bush 3 or 4 feet high in shrub borders. Bean in *Shrubs and Trees Hardy in The British Isles* mentions a specimen growing 15 feet high on the wall of a house near the main entrance to Kew Botanic Gardens. It is completely hardy. It does not appear to be listed in any current catalogues.

J. nudiflorum (naked-flowering; the flowers come on leafless shoots). This is the best known and the best loved of all the Jasmines – I think many people prefer it even to the common white, fragrant species. Cottage walls are often covered with it, and it will begin blooming in November and continue till March. I don't know of a better place for it than a wall facing north. The flowers are nearly always spoiled during a severe spell when the plant is grown in the open garden. Even in thin woodland it can be badly damaged. Give it a wall for the sake of its bright yellow winter flowers. They hardly need describing; they are about 1 inch wide and come singly on the long growths made during the summer months. The leaves, small and 3-foliolate, follow the flowers.

If one or two stems are left to trail on the ground, they will root very readily without being pegged down.

The species was discovered in China by Robert Fortune and introduced in 1844. It was first thought to be tender and recommended as a good greenhouse shrub. But Fortune later described it as being perfectly hardy. "It was first discovered in gardens and nurseries in the north of China, particularly about Shanghai, Loo-chou, and Nanking. . . . It is deciduous; the leaves falling off in its native country early in autumn, and leaving a number of large, prominent flower-buds, which expand in early spring, often when the snow is on the ground, and look like little primroses."

J. officinale (literally 'kept at the druggist's shop'. The epithet is common enough and usually refers to the roots, stems and leaves of plants which are used medicinally. An essential oil, reddish-brown in colour, is distilled from the flowers of several species of Jasmine).

The Common Jasmine or *Jessamine*, the oldest of all our decorative climbers. L. H. Bailey, describing it as a plant for American gardens, calls it a long, slender grower needing support, but scarcely self-climbing. "With protection it will stand as far as North Philadelphia."

In our country it is mostly grown on walls (near windows, because of its scent) or over the arches of doorways. And in these places it needs support: trellis or wires may be used. It may also be grown in the open garden in warm districts: left to trail its long shoots (these grow 6 feet or more in a season) over shrubs or hedges. It will twine round slender stems and twigs and go up to a good height; trained on a wall, it reaches 30 or 40 feet. Kept to bush shape, about 6 feet, it is pretty in summer; and I have seen it used for a low hedge, several plants being set in a longish row. They make so much untidy growth round the base, that a good, dense hedge is soon formed. Too drastic pruning and cutting back, however, will prevent it from flowering freely; and it is on a high wall that it is seen at its best. Stephen Miller (1691–1771) says in his famous *Dictionary* that "plants should be permitted to grow rude in the summer, otherwise there will be no flowers; but after the summer is past the luxuriant shoots must be pruned off. . . ."

The taller a specimen grows, the more profusely it flowers. It need not be pruned much on an archway, where the long stems will fall over the other side, or on a pergola, where they can be taken across the roofing cross-beams.

It is chiefly for its scent that the *Jessamine* is grown. The flowers, small, measuring about $\frac{7}{8}$ inch long and as much across the lobes, come on longish stalks in clusters of from three to eight. The leaves are composed of 5, 7 or 9 leaflets, dark green in colour and usually fall in the autumn. In warm regions they appear to be semi-evergreen.

The species is native to Persia, North-west India and China. Miller also gives Malabar (South-west India), where "it grows naturally"; it has been found at altitudes of from 3,000–9,000 feet in Kashmir.

There are one or two varieties offered by nurseries: var. *affine*, with larger flowers, more numerous in the cyme or cluster; and var. *aureum*, whose foliage is blotched with yellow. I have never grown these or any of the others, but they are less hardy than the type plant. Miller recommended covering them with "mats or straw to prevent their being killed".

The very fragrant *J. grandiflora* (large flowers) is given as a variety by some botanists. Its flowers are similar to those of *J. officinale* but larger and reddish beneath. It is quite tender and must be grown in a hot-house in this country. Usually planted in a pot, it makes a straggling but attractive bush which blooms almost continuously. It is the species whose flowers are mostly used for making the valuable Jasmine oil.

J. polyanthum (many-flowered: free-flowering). This is a

very beautiful Jasmine but unfortunately on the tender side and therefore in most districts best grown in a cool greenhouse. Nonetheless it does give a remarkably good show in our warmest, maritime counties, especially if it is trained up a wall. It is a climber, usually evergreen, and will go up to a good height if given a suitable place. The pinnate leaves are from 3 to 5 inches long, the leaflets numbering 5 or 7; and the flowers come in panicles 2 to 4 inches in length. Often 20 or 30 flowers are carried in a single panicle; these are delightfully fragrant, white within and rose-coloured on the outside; they measure about $\frac{3}{4}$ inch across the top of the corolla. They are usually at their best in midsummer and in the South start to open much earlier.

Specimens that are trained up walls must be supported by trellis-work or by wires. In exceptionally warm, sheltered gardens the plant may be grown on a shrub; it will weave its way up to the top and look remarkably attractive when the panicles of pinkish-white flowers hang down from the branches.

Similarly, in a cool greenhouse, it may be grown up trellis fixed to the wall or given a slender twig or two to weave itself round, the latter being set firmly in the pot or tub when the Jasmine is planted.

The species comes from Yunnan, China, where Père Delavay discovered it in 1883. Forrest saw it in full bloom in the Tali valley during the summer months of 1906 and also came across it at high altitudes on the eastern flank of the Tali Range.

It may be got from most shrub specialists. Marchant's describes it as a "fast-growing, semi-evergreen climber for milder districts. Flowers white, rosy outside, very sweetly scented and borne from June to September."

J. primulinum (primrose-like: Hillier's catalogue describes it as the "Primrose Jasmine"). The semi-double primrose-yellow flowers somewhat resemble the old-fashioned double Primrose.

The species is as tender as the preceding and on that account more often grown in a greenhouse than outside. Although tried against a warm south wall at Kew, it has repeatedly succumbed to frosts. In the South of France and in Italy it flourishes luxuriantly. L. H. Bailey in *The Standard Cyclopedia of Horticulture* says that in the U.S.A., "it stands some frost . . . blooms in early spring, the season lasting two months or more.

Not hardy north of Washington, and nearly evergreen in the South."

Grown in the open (in the south) it makes a rambling shrub up to about 10 feet high. On a wall, where it needs training and pruning into shape, it will reach a height of 15 feet and be beautiful in spring with its uncommon yellow flowers. These are like those of the Winter Jasmine but larger and much more attractive. They are often double; the corolla is about $1\frac{1}{2}$ inches long and has from 6 to 10 lobes, which give a wonderfully rich effect. The diameter of the individual flower is roughly $1\frac{1}{2}$ inches. The evergreen leaves, a perfect foil to the flowers, are composed of 3 leaflets 1 to 3 inches long. If we could get it to grow outside in this country, no doubt we should plant it in preference to the Winter Jasmine. It is often compared with that species, but *J. primulinum* is a superior plant. However, if we want to grow it, we can do so by planting it in a pot; and this is often done. A 12-inch pot, well drained and filled with a good rich loam, is required, and it should be set against a warm, sunny wall where the plant will come into blossom about April. It needs feeding when the flower-buds begin to show (give it an occasional dose of weak liquid manure, say, every 10 days until they are fully open) and house it as soon as the weather turns cold.

This loveliest of all Jasmines is obtainable from most shrub nurseries. Marchant's describes it as "The most beautiful of all outdoor Jasmines but not quite hardy, though worthy of a warm, sheltered wall. The $1\frac{1}{2}$–2 in. soft yellow flowers are freely borne from May to early autumn."

At Truro (near the coast of Cornwall) there is a magnificent specimen which covers the wall of a house and is in full bloom during March.

J. × *stephanense* (the plant was raised in 1918 by Messrs. Lemoine & Sons of Nancy).

This Jasmine is a hybrid between *J. beesianum* and *J. officinale* and has charming pale pink fragrant flowers. Although it has been in cultivation half a century, it is not often seen in our gardens. Its flowers are more freely carried than those of *J. beesianum* and more showy than those of *J. officinale*. They come in clusters, the individual flower has a slender corolla $\frac{1}{2}$ inch long and measures as much across the rounded lobes. Around

London the flowers begin to open in June and last till about mid-July. The plant is as hardy as the Bees Jasmine and I have seen it grown in conjunction with the Common White Jasmine on an arch; it goes up as high as that species and the two look very attractive together. It could be similarly grown on a pergola. On a wall it needs a trellis or supporting wires. It may be seen in June covering a wall at Wisley with its clusters of pretty pink flowers.

The leaves are sometimes simple and ovalish as in the Bees plant, and sometimes pinnate, with 5 leaflets, as in the other parent; they are a dull green, slightly downy beneath and show up the flowers well, when they retain their attractive green; but unfortunately they have a tendency to variegation.

Many gardeners aver that it is the black, glossy berries which come abundantly in autumn which make it a valuable climber – its flowers are pretty but not striking.

It is obtainable from most shrub specialists. Hillier describes it as a vigorous climber, bearing fragrant, pale pink flowers.

Although several Jasmines are described as vigorous climbers, they all need some assistance in their early stages of growth. It is best to provide *J. officinale*, for example, with a thin bamboo cane, round which it can twine when it is planted near a porch which it is ultimately to cover. The ideal structure for it would be a trellis made of these thin bamboos, the shoots being trained, or finding their own way, up them. In the open garden it needs the thin slender twigs of a bush: not the thick trunk of a tree. It has been known, however, to pile up in a loose untidy mass, twisting and twining its long growths round one another against an old apple-tree, till they reached up high enough to grasp a slender branch.

[3]

Honeysuckle is a native climber and, like the Jasmine, a twiner which in shady places sends up its long stems towards the light. You may see it in our woods; and where it stands alone, it is bush-like and upright in its young state and, if finding nothing to clamber over or climb up, will eventually make a straggling mass of stems. It is the first woody plant to come into leaf; often in January its pale green shoots will be conspicuous among the bare deciduous trees.

Lonicera periclymenum is the name of the native plant (another species, *L. caprifolium* is said to be indigenous); it is also found in other parts of Europe, and in North Africa and Asia Minor. Of all our native plants, this, the Woodbine, is undoubtedly the most beautiful and probably the first ornamental climber to be cultivated in our gardens.

Linnaeus named the genus in honour of the German naturalist Adam Lonicer, 1528–86. Honeysuckle is the common name of the climbing section; and the name was also used in the Middle Ages for various plants whose flowers yielded honey or nectar. Clovers, red and white, were often referred to as Honeysuckles. In the seventeenth century a writer described a field where the grass was full of "honie suckles both red and white". The earliest quotation given by the *O.E.D.* is 1256: "Ligustrum (privet) triffoil, hunisuccles." It is occasionally used too in conjunction with another word for certain shrubs or plants whose fragrance is reminiscent of the Honeysuckle's. The Purple Honeysuckle is *Rhododendron nudiflorum*; White Honeysuckle *Rhododendron viscosum*; and False Honeysuckle refers to some of the sweet-scented Azaleas. The Bush Honeysuckles are of course the shrub *Lonicera*; some are partly scandent and when planted against a wall will go up to a good height.

'Woodbine' is less used nowadays for the native climber and indeed the word is unknown to many people. It refers naturally to the twining nature of the climber as it binds itself round stems and branches. The name was formerly 'Woodbind'. The *O.E.D.* quotes Pilkington (1562), who says, "The woodbinde climbes up and spreads it selfe over all the branches, unto it has overgrowen and kylled the hole tree."

I have never seen a tree killed by it in this country. But *L. ciliosa*, a native of North America, is a notorious strangler and has been known to kill many trees in the woods of South Carolina (see page 52).

Fine specimens of *L. caprifolium* grow in the Hampshire woods (probably escapes from gardens) and have bound themselves tightly round branches. When the twisting stems are uncoiled or cut away, the indentations or furrows in the bark are clearly visible. Both this climber and the Woodbine are beautifully figured (Plate 98, Vol. 3) in *Flowering Plants of Great Britain* by Anne Pratt.

The Woodbine is listed in some catalogues but rarely offered for sale, the varieties such as the Early Dutch Honeysuckle and the Late Dutch Honeysuckle being favoured by most gardeners.

The genus *Lonicera* belongs to the Family *Caprifolium*, and consists of about 180 species, bushy or climbing plants, deciduous and evergreen. They have a wide distribution in the Northern Hemisphere: from North America to Mexico; and in Asia as far south as Java. We are fortunate in having such a richly fragrant and floriferous species as a native plant – I think it superior to many from abroad. Some species are scentless, though their flowers are very striking and delightfully coloured. (*L. sempervirens* is one of the loveliest); and some are tender, such as *L. hildebrandiana*, and need housing.

The shrubby species we are not discussing, but there are one or two that are best grown against a warm wall, as they bloom in the winter; and in such a place will grow tall and smell even more sweetly. These are included with the rarer climbers and wall plants in chapter three.

Many have small and quite insignificant flowers: of a yellowish-cream colour which hardly shows up against the foliage. These shrubs when planted in woodland or against a group of tall bushes will spread out and make an excellent screen. I bought *L. xerocalyx* many years ago as a screening shrub. In Dorset and other warm regions it is extremely vigorous, growing like a big climber; but it remains quite a dwarf in this part of the country (Bucks.), and is hardly worth planting.

The genus has been divided into three Sections, viz. (1) *Periclymenum* (the name is the specific epithet of the native climber): twining plants, one of their characters being the collar-like effect of the joined leaves at the tops of the stems (though in *L. periclymenum* itself the leaves are not joined). (2) *Xylosteum* (the specific epithet of a bush *Lonicera* thought to be wild in the South of England): bush Honeysuckles; their leaves are never united as in the preceding group. (3) *Nintooa* (from *Nin Too*, the Japanese name of *Lonicera japonica*): twining plants, mostly evergreen (like *L. japonica*, which represents the group in cultivation); the leaves are never united.

D

Honeysuckles of all types need rich loamy soil and a moist root-run. When they are planted in full sun, they are never a success. It is only necessary to look at any specimen of the Woodbine growing in the hedges to see why it blooms so profusely. The base or the lower stems are not visible; these are usually deep in a thicket of Blackthorn or some other wilding; the long twining stems easily work their way round the twiggy, prickly branches and reach the top and often go up a height of 20 or 30 feet or more in search of the sun. It is not difficult to provide the plants with similar conditions in the garden. Dwarf shrubs may be planted in front of them or round them to shade the ground in which they grow. Or large boulders may be sunk in the soil at suitable points and will provide not only shade but keep the soil moist throughout the year.

The following climbing Honeysuckles are listed in most catalogues. Several will be found in our gardens · and all of them may be seen in nurseries and Botanic Collections; the tender *L. hildebrandiana* is magnificent in the Temperate House at Kew.

L. × *brownii*. (Named in honour of Dr. Robert Brown, F.R.S., the eminent English botanist.) This is a hybrid from *L. sempervirens* and *L. hirsuta*, both North American species. From them it inherits its hardiness and, alas, its scentless flowers. They are, however, beautifully coloured orange and scarlet and a wonderful sight on a mature plant. The scarlet tubular part measures 1½ inches long; the lip and inside, or throat, are orange. The glaucous green leaves, 1½ to 3½ inches long, contrast strikingly with the brilliantly-coloured flowers. This Honeysuckle begins blooming in May and goes on to the autumn. It is a deciduous twiner which is completely hardy in many parts of the country and, like most of the genus, does best in a cool soil and a shady spot. Its popular name is the Scarlet Trumpet Honeysuckle. Hillier's catalogue (1955–56) lists *L.* × *brownii fuchsioides*: "Bears its glowing orange-scarlet flowers early and late. With semi-evergreen foliage and of moderate vigour." The varieties *fuchsioides*; *plantierensis*; *punicea*; and *youngii* are similar and of the same origin. All are hardy and similarly coloured.

L. caprifolium (the word is an old Latin name for Honeysuckle: *caper*, goat; *folium*, leaf; goats apparently used to feed on the foliage of the wild plants). It was at one time thought to be a native of this country. It is found growing up to great heights in woodlands south of London; but its indigenousness is now doubted; the plants are probably naturalized or escapes from gardens. In parts of Europe it is a common wild twiner; in the U.S.A. it is also an escape.

Often the plants are not visible, their flowers being hidden among the foliage among which they grow; but their rich scent betrays their whereabouts. The scent is always strongest at night; and it has been observed that it attracts the Convolvulus Hawk-moth which can smell the flowers at a great distance away. It has been said that most Honeysuckles smell strongest "from 6 or 7 in the evening till midnight".

The species is deciduous, like the common native plant, and very much like it in appearance, the flowers, yellowish-white and red, coming in whorls at the ends of the shoots. It may be distinguished from the other, however, in the character of its leaves: already referred to (page 49). The terminal leaves are united at the base. Those immediately below are quite separate

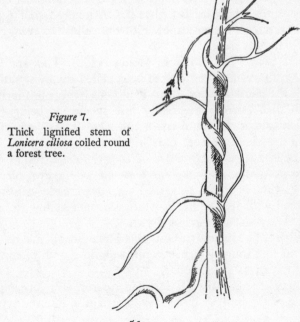

Figure 7.
Thick lignified stem of *Lonicera ciliosa* coiled round a forest tree.

but stalkless; and below these they have short stalks. In *L. periclymenum* the leaves are never united.

L. caprifolium appears in most catalogues. Hillier's describes it: "Flowers creamy-white, fragrant, borne profusely in June and July. Sometimes known as the 'Early Cream'."

L. ciliosa (with ciliate leaves: the margins fringed with hairs). Indigenous to western North America; very seldom seen in our gardens now; it was introduced in 1824. In cultivation it is a moderate-sized twiner and suitable for training on a trellis up a north or a north-west wall. Grown in this way, the shoots twine round the narrow slats and the whole structure in a year or two will be a mass of glaucous green leaves and orange-scarlet and yellow flowers.

In its native habitat this deciduous Honeysuckle is much more vigorous. Trees in South Carolina have been strangled by it, the thick rope-like coiling stems working their way into the bark, causing it to dry up, which ultimately kills the tree. The popular name of the plant is the Western Trumpet Honeysuckle.

Opinions on its hardiness differ. It has been called one of the hardiest, a popular Honeysuckle in parts of northern Germany. Marchant's catalogue describes it: "A lovely twining plant for a sheltered, semi-shady spot. Flowers yellow to orange-scarlet. Not generally hardy."

L. etrusca (The Etruscan Honeysuckle). This species from the Mediterranean region has been called the most satisfactory of all the climbing kinds. But it blooms freely not much farther north than Surrey; the really fine specimens being found in gardens along the south and south-west coasts, and, of course, along the Mediterranean coast-line.

The leaves resemble those of *L. caprifolium*; the flowers are more gorgeous, I think – at least on well-grown plants. The corolla-tube is about 2 inches long, of a creamy-yellow colour suffused with red, which becomes a deeper yellow in late summer. The scent is heavy and rich.

Where the climate suits it, this Honeysuckle makes growths several feet long, which become weighted with blossom. It is ideal for a cool greenhouse.

There are several varieties: var. *superba*, with larger panicles, is one of the best. It flourishes luxuriantly, like the type plant, in a cool greenhouse; and I have seen it in the Temperate House at Kew. C. H. Wright describes that specimen in Vol. LX of the *Botanical Magazine*. *L. etrusca* var. *superba* "flowered in the Himalayan section of the Temperate House at Kew in August, 1903. The plant was purchased from a continental nurseryman about ten years previously. The conditions in this situation are eminently favourable for it, and its stem has attained a diameter of 2 inches, and its shoots grow from 6 to 10 feet in length in a season. These shoots bear, for a distance of several feet from the apex, numerous short, lateral branches terminated by the cluster of flowers, and, hanging down from the rafters, present the appearance of a graceful cloud of colour. In the open air the plant also thrives, but does not flower so freely as indoors. It is easily propagated from cuttings."

L. giraldii (in honour of Père Giuseppe Girald, Italian missionary and naturalist in China, 1890).

This is an evergreen twiner from Szechwan, China. A striking Honeysuckle of moderate growth in our gardens, where it needs a warm but shady wall. The purplish-red and yellowish flower-clusters are small but very charming and carried abundantly. In its young state the plant is clothed with erect yellow hairs, which add to its attraction.

It needs a wall in most districts and is prized as a cool greenhouse climber. In the autumn it bears clusters of purplish black berries.

It came to this country from France, where it was introduced in 1899. Most shrub specialists stock it. Hillier lists it: "Evergreen, Chinese twining species, soon becoming a dense mass of intertwining branches. Flowers purplish-red, rather small, but numerous." The species belongs to the *Nintooa* Section.

L. × heckrottii. Dr. Rehder in his Monograph *Synopsis of the Genus Lonicera* says he has not been able to learn anything about the origin of this hybrid and suggests that *L. sempervirens* and *L. italica* (*L. × italica*) are its parents. It is completely hardy and although not strictly speaking a climber, is often planted against a wall and supported by wires. From June to August its flowers, carried in terminal spikes, are very attractive with their orange-yellow and pink colouring. They are fragrant and show up well against the glaucous green foliage. This hybrid originated in America and was offered there for some years before it arrived in Britain. Marchant's catalogue describes it, "A hybrid with oblong leaves, glaucous beneath, and striking 1½ inch orange-yellow and pink flowers from June to autumn frosts. Not a fast grower and averse to full sun." The parentage is given as *sempervirens* × *americana*; × *americana* is the hybridal epithet now used by many botanists instead of × *italica*.

L. henryi has been discarded by many nurseries as it is considered an unsatisfactory garden plant, Hillier's list it in their 1955–56 catalogue. I have included it because it is evergreen and quite attractive in the autumn months with its crop of bluish-black berries. Its purplish-red flowers are not showy and do not vie with those of the other Honeysuckles described here; but its dark, glossy green foliage is a cheerful sight throughout the winter months; and if the plant, which is a vigorous climber, is trained up a trellis against a wall, it provides an excellent background for flowers and dwarf shrubs. A native of China and Tibet, it was introduced by Wilson in 1908.

The species was named for Augustine Henry, who had previously collected it in the province of Hupeh, China.

Its value as an evergreen climber is commented upon in the *Botanical Magazine* (Tab. 8175): "The fact that the species is evergreen gives it a particular value in gardens, for in spite of the quite extraordinary number of hardy woody plants that have been introduced during the last decade, true evergreen climbers, as distinguished from the hardy shrubs made to do duty as such on garden walls, form still but a small group. This is largely due to the fact that evergreen climbers represent a type of vegetation more characteristic of tropical and subtropical than of the cool temperate zones."

L. hildebrandiana (named in honour of A. H. Hildebrand, Esq., who presented Kew Botanic Gardens with the first specimen).

The largest of all the climbing species; its common name is the Giant Honeysuckle. It is not possible to grow it in many gardens unfortunately, for it is tender and will not survive a severe frost. Good flowering specimens may be seen outside in our warmest, maritime counties such as Cornwall and Devon; and Bean mentions a plant that belonged to the late Reverend H. Ewbank, which flowered on a west wall at Ryde, Isle of Wight.

And the species flourishes luxuriantly in the south and west of Ireland, where many tender plants succeed.

It is a Honeysuckle that every lover of the genus should see; there is a fine specimen in the Temperate House at Kew, which grows up to the roof and is at its best about June. The leaves, usually evergreen, are 3 to 6 inches long and 2 to 4 inches wide; the creamy-white, fragrant flowers (deepening to orange as they age) come in pairs, the tubular part is often 6 inches long and 3 inches across the top, or lips. A magnificent flower. And no doubt the plant is a spectacle when seen in full bloom in its habitat. It climbs to a height of 60 to 80 feet.

Those who can grow it, should give it a place where its upper stems can be in full sunlight and the roots in shady moist soil. It seldom flowers freely in cultivation in its young state.

Sir Henry Collett first discovered it in 1888 on the Shan Hills in Burma. Augustine Henry found it also in Yunnan, China; and it is common in Siam.

Collett was told that the flowers are much used for decorating temples in Burma and that their colour was crimson. Apparently the colour varies somewhat in different plants. There is a specimen at the Botanical Gardens at Glasnevin, Dublin, whose flowers are a soft yellow when they open; this becomes darker and is finally a reddish-orange. On the Kew plant the buds are white, tinged with pink; the open flower a golden-buff, which turns yellow-brown with age.

L. × *italica* (from Italy). This deciduous climber is a hybrid between *L. caprifolium* and *L. etrusca*. It is thought to be a natural hybrid; and plants have been found growing wild in southern Europe. The hybrid is usually described now as *L.* × *americana* and appears under this name in most catalogues. Specimens found in North America are escapes from gardens.

The plant has been praised for its early flowering habit and its rich smell. It is in fact regarded as the richest of all the Honeysuckle scents and can at times be almost overpowering, especially after a warm summer shower. The flowers are yellow stained with reddish-purple and come in loose panicles 12 inches or more long.

Marchant's catalogue describes the plant as a natural hybrid. "Undoubtedly one of the very best climbers and one of the most neglected."

The various forms of *L.* × *italica* do not appear to be listed in any catalogue. There are var. *quercifolia*, with leaves shaped like those of an Oak; var. *rubella*, with pale purple flowers; and var. *atrosanguinea*, with dark red-purple flowers, which is the most striking.

L. japonica (Japanese). A useful and very fragrant evergreen Honeysuckle, one of the most rampant in places which suit it. In my garden it has smothered several old shrubs and killed some of the branches round which it is twined. When they break off after a gale, as often happens, it is difficult to unwind the stems to release the dead branches.

This species makes plenty of new growths, the long shoots falling to the ground when they have nothing to twine round. They root there and the new stem rises and twists and turns in search of a supporting twig. They are hairy and eventually climb to a height of 30 feet. The flowers, yellowish, come in pairs in the leaf-axils and bloom from June till late September.

The variety *Halliana* is perhaps better known and more often seen in gardens. It has smallish white flowers which turn deep yellow as they age.

The great attraction of these *japonica* Honeysuckles is their fragrance which continues so long through the year.

Two other varieties are offered by nurseries; these are var. *aureo-reticulata* (yellow-veined); the veins and midrib of the leaves are bright yellow. Var. *flexuosa* (tortuous, bending); long reddish-purple shoots and flowers pale purple outside.

People who garden around London have found these *japonica* Honeysuckles not always completely hardy, the bright green leaves sometimes being badly shrivelled and blackened by frosts. One or two unlucky people have actually lost their plants during a severe winter. It may be slightly tender in its youth, but it grows well as a rule after it has been established for a few years.

The habitat of *L. japonica* is Japan, Korea and China. It was introduced into Britain in 1806.

L. periclymenum (an old Latin name for the Wild Honeysuckle, Woodbine; it was also called *clymenus*). The native Honeysuckle which we see on our hedges in midsummer and growing over tall Blackthorns; occasionally it tops a tall tree and lets down its stems laden with blossom. The scent is one of the delights of the English countryside; and it is always strongest in the evening or very early in the morning. The wild Honeysuckle can be transplanted from the hedgerows to the garden, though, rightly, this would be frowned on, for it is among the most valuable of all our wildings. There are several forms of it offered for sale by nurseries and on the whole they do better in gardens than the wild type. Bean recommends var. *belgica* and var. *serotina* as better plants.

The first, popularly known as the Early Dutch Honeysuckle, has flowers purplish-red without, becoming paler; and yellow within; it blooms fairly early and is more bushy in habit than the wild kind.

Var. *serotina*, the Late Dutch Honeysuckle, is similar in its colouring; its leaves are often variegated. There is another called var. *quercina*, whose leaves are lobed like those of the Oak-tree; the flowers are smaller than those of the type and purple inside.

These twiners are particularly beautiful climbing over bushes or small trees. If they are planted on a wall, they should be given a shady one. My experience with them is that they do best in a woodland and bloom there more freely than anywhere else.

L. sempervirens (ever green) is one of the tender Honeysuckles, suitable only for a few gardens in this country. It grows well and flowers freely in south-west Ireland and in places with soft, warm climates. It is best housed in most districts in England. Not many nurseries stock the plant: Marchant's state that it "needs wall protection". The flowers come in June and go on to September and are exceptionally showy with their scarlet and yellow colouring but unfortunately they have no scent.

The leaves, evergreen in warm countries, are a rich bluish-green and show off the vivid colour of the flowers magnificently.

This vigorous evergreen twiner is the most showy of the North American species and a native of the south-eastern States. It was introduced into Britain as long ago as 1656 and cultivated by the famous botanist, John Tradescant, Jun., in that year. Its tenderness, however, prevents the species from being widely grown in our gardens. The hybrids derived from it – *L.* × *brownii*, *L.* × *heckrottii*, for example – are hardy and consequently much better known.

Those who have a warm, shady wall and can provide some winter protection, should give the plant a trial for it is very beautiful. Its popular name is the Trumpet Honeysuckle. It belongs to the *Periclymenum* Section and is usually propagated by layering the young branches.

L. similis delavayi. (The species is listed in some books as *L. delavayi* – named for the French botanist Delavay – this specific name, however, being now used as a synonym. The plant was named *Caprifolium simile*[1] by Kuntze in 1891.) It is an evergreen or semi-evergreen Honeysuckle and belongs to the *Japonica* group. Remarkable for the abundance of flowers it carries in August. It is about the last to bloom. The flowers, delightfully fragrant, with long, very slender tubular corollas, are cream-coloured at first and then a bright lemon-yellow. They produce a light, foamy effect, which is set off beautifully by the glaucous green foliage. It is a fine Honeysuckle for training over a warm, shady porch, the flowers falling over the arch and making a charming picture for the early autumn. It needs a protected spot such as this, for its shoots, which develop rather late, are often damaged by frost.

The Abbé Delavay discovered the species in Yunnan, China, in 1888; it was introduced into France in 1901 and to Kew in 1907, the plants coming from the famous nurseries of Mr. Maurice de Vilmorin. Most shrub specialists have the plant and describe it as a valuable evergreen climber and quite hardy. It is propagated by late summer cuttings.

L. splendida (showy, shining). It is commonly known as the Spanish Honeysuckle and is a native of Spain, where it is evergreen and a vigorous twining plant which climbs over bushes, covering them with purplish flowers in June. In places which suit it, it makes growths as much as 6 feet in a season; unfortunately it has proved rather difficult under cultivation. Hillier's list it as tender and describe it as "A beautiful and distinct but fastidious Spanish species, at once recognized by its blue-green leaves".

With its fragrant, purplish flowers, yellowish within, and its blue-green foliage, it is one of the loveliest members of the

[1] *similis*, having a likeness to another species.

family. The flowers come in terminal, stalkless spikes and are at their best from June to August. People living in warm, maritime districts have found that the plant flourishes in their gardens and needs no winter protection.

There is a good specimen growing outside at Kew; it is planted on the south wall of the Temperate House and flowers well in that position.

L. × *tellmanniana.* This deciduous hybrid Honeysuckle is completely hardy and was raised in the Royal Hungarian Horticultural School, Budapest, the parent plants being *L. tragophylla* and *L. sempervirens* var. superba. The long, trumpet-shaped corollas, with their protruding stamens, are a glowing yellow touched at the tips with bronzy-red. A striking flower; the clusters giving a wonderfully decorative effect. It is a scentless Honeysuckle but much admired for all that. Many nurseries stock it and recommend it for most districts; it is quite hardy, though it seems to bloom more freely in gardens around London when planted on a shady wall. It needs a good rich loam.

L. tragophylla (Greek: *tragos*, goat; *phyllon*, leaves – with leaves like those of *L. caprifolium*; see the species, page 50).

Like the preceding plant, this Honeysuckle is scentless but, with its enormous clusters of bright yellow flowers, ranks among the most decorative. It is known as the great Chinese Woodbine and comes from the province of Hupeh, where it was discovered by Henry. Wilson introduced it for Messrs. Veitch in 1900. He found it climbing over bushes in mountainous regions at altitudes of from 4,000 to 7,500 feet. It is known to the Chinese as the *Ta-chin-yin-hua* (Great Gold and Silver Flower). Unfortunately we seldom see it in our gardens; no doubt most people prefer the fragrant kinds – though in flower they are not so striking as this plant.

In gardens where it has settled down (it likes to ramble over tall shrubs best) it goes up to a height of 20 feet or more and will give a glorious show of blossom in midsummer. The clusters have from 10 to 20 blooms, the tubular part being about 3 inches long and 1 inch across the lobes or lip. The flowers almost equal those of the Giant Honeysuckle (*L. hildebrandiana*) in size. They contrast beautifully with the glaucous green leaves, which measure about 4 inches long and are half as wide; the uppermost pair are united at the base.

As regards culture: the best flowering specimens I have seen have been growing freely over bushes; it certainly does not like a sunny wall, but will grow well if planted against the shady side and trained to trail over in the sun.

Ernest Markham who grows it says, "Not infrequently the plant will suddenly collapse for no apparent reason, its only failing known to me."

It is propagated readily by cuttings; these if half woody will root out of doors. Most shrub specialists have the plant for sale.

Most gardeners prefer to propagate their Honeysuckles by taking the firmer cuttings and inserting them in sandy soil out of doors. It is the easiest, hardy, method. Cuttings about 4 inches long with a heel are taken in July or August and left covered with a bell-glass in a shady place till they are rooted.

Gardeners who have a heated greenhouse can use softer shoots; these are inserted in damp sand and given gentle bottom heat. They root in a few weeks.

Seeds are sometimes sown (in a warm greenhouse in March); but as the *Lonicera* hybridize very readily, only the seed of isolated specimens should be taken.

As regards pests that attack Honeysuckles: most people are acquainted with *Lonicera* Aphis: it is unfortunately very common. Some kinds appear to be more susceptible to it than others. I have never seen my specimens of *L. japonica* affected with it; but many species and varieties belonging to the *Periclymenum* Section are. The leaves are usually attacked; the pests causing them to curl up and permanently disfiguring them. They are not easy to reach with a solution; but nicotine dust penetrates into the rolled leaf and destroys them. When the aphides are visible, spraying with a nicotine-soap wash is best.

Honeysuckles growing against walls, especially those with a hot, sunny aspect, are nearly always affected. In shade and where the soil is moist, the plants usually escape.

On the whole it is best not to use any shrub or tree we value as a support for vigorous twining plants. Some, like *Lonicera ciliosa*, already referred to, may strangle it by the pressure exerted by the coiling twisting stems. These thicken and lignify and in this woody state prevent the trunk of the tree from developing naturally and subsequently cause its death. Most of the Honeysuckles we grow, however, do little damage to trees.

Old well-established specimens of our native Honeysuckle and its varieties (the most common kinds seen in our gardens) often form thick woody stems which scarcely twine, the upper shoots twisting round thin branches or whatever is accessible and keeping the plants securely in place. Fig. 7, page 51, shows the thick, lignified stems of *L. ciliosa*.

[4]

THE Rose Family contains many ornamental climbers which are among the showiest we can grow. There are the Wild Roses or species, which make their way up trees and through tall bushes by means of long, spiny shoots (*Rosa gigantea*, tender, goes up to a height of 40 feet); and, more popular, the hybrid climbers and ramblers (often with double flowers) which are derived from some of the species. On walls they need support, like the Honeysuckles; and trellis is usually provided for them.

The genus is *Rosa*, the name being an old Latin word for the Rose. In most ancient civilizations when man has gardened, the Rose has been cultivated. And no doubt it is most people's favourite flower.

Probably the first roses grown in our gardens were introduced by the Romans, who brought with them many of the plants, ornamental and economic, that we cultivate.

The famous *Rosa damascena* var. *bifera* (the Four Seasons' Rose) was grown in their gardens. It was apparently used on a lavish scale for adorning the banqueting halls of the Emperor Nero. (The plant is obtainable from shrub specialists.) *R. damascena* (the Damask Rose) is a native of Asia Minor and regarded by some botanists as a natural variation of another ancient species called *R. gallica*, whose provenance is lost in the darkness of antiquity. It appeared among other flowers in the wall paintings at the palace of Knossos, Crete, which dates back to the Minoan civilization – about 2000 B.C. Another ancient rose, *R. gallica versicolor*, is listed in many catalogues as *Rosa Mundi* (a synonym) and is still prized by rosarians for its flowers. They are rose-red striped with white, but sometimes all the flowers are of a self red. It is not the genuine York and Lancaster

Rose of historical fame. This famous and very lovely rose is *R. damascena* var. *versicolor* and is listed by Hillier's as the *York and Lancaster*; a few years ago it cost 5s. 6d. per plant.

None of these old roses, however, are climbers (*R. damascena* goes up to a height of 8 feet and is very effective spread out on a wooden trellis). They are important because they were among the first to be grown in this country and from them come some of the popular garden varieties. They have their economic value, too; in southern countries where they prosper exceedingly, some of them, *R. damascena* var. *trigintipetala* particularly, are cultivated on a large scale for the essential oil, Attar of Roses, which is distilled from the flowers.

It was not till about the seventeenth century that the first climbers were brought to this country. *R. sempervirens*, with small, white flowers, slightly fragrant, was one of the first. It is native to southern Europe and North-west Africa, but I doubt if it is now in cultivation. (Its hybrids are wonderful and widely grown.) It is not among the best of the climbers but is mentioned because it points to *R. wichuraiana*, which is related to it and which has produced such beautiful ramblers as 'Dorothy Perkins', 'Excelsa' and 'Albéric Barbier'.

We must not of course forget the native Wild Rose, *R. canina* (the Dog Rose), which goes up to a height of 12 feet or so and has charming white or pinkish flowers. It is one of the loveliest of our native plants and may sometimes be seen in fields, where it makes a straggling bushy plant about 6 feet high, covered with flowers in June. In the hedgerows its long growths push their way up twice this height.

R. bracteata, introduced by Lord Macartney from China in 1793, is among the best of the tall-growing species and produced that superb climber 'Mermaid', which was acclaimed the finest of all climbing roses when it appeared about 1918. I do not think it has ever been eclipsed.

Hillier's catalogue lists the plant and rightly states that it needs a warm wall and good soil. Most shrub specialists have a selection of climbing rose species. They should be grown in gardens as they grow in nature: climbing over bushes and up trees.

The genus contains all types of plants: dwarfs, bushes and tall climbers. About 125 species are recognized: 95 are Asiatic;

18 American; and the rest are distributed in Europe and North-west Africa. Several are indigenous to Britain. They are all native to the northern hemisphere. None is found in the southern half of the world. The following are some of the love-liest and can be got from most shrub nurseries.

R. × *alba* (white) is considered to be a hybrid between *R. canina* and *R. damascena*. This rose and its various forms are delightfully fragrant and worth growing for their scent alone – it has been compared to the sharp smell of eau-de-Cologne. They are not tall growers but suitable for training on a trellis against a wall; they are seen to best advantage there, as the flowers are held upright. Twisted round pillars (as I have sometimes seen these plants) they do not display the beauty of the flowers very well. The *alba* roses are hardy enough to be grown in most parts of the country and thrive in shade: on a north or an east wall.

The flowers, about 3 inches across, are single or double and come in clusters; they are at their best in early summer. And the silvery or greyish foliage makes the plants attractive when they are not in bloom. In the autumn they bear bright red heps.

Of the different forms grown in our gardens, var. *alba* 'Celestial', with semi-double, delicate rose-pink flowers, is a special favourite; the leaves, cupped and having an attractive metallic sheen, distinguish the plant from the others.

Var. *alba* 'Maiden's Blush' has very double, pale pink, sweetly-smelling flowers and bluish-green foliage – a lovely plant on trellis on a north wall, where the light is rather sub-dued. For my part I prefer the double-white flowers of the type plant. The roses seen in the pictures of the Renaissance painters are these exquisitely-shaped flowers. The popular name of the flower is The White Rose of York, or the Jacobite Rose.

The alba roses are strong-growing plants and flourish in any ordinary garden soil.

R. × *anemonoides* (anemone-shaped flowers). It is a hybrid between *R. laevigata* and probably *R. odorata* and often appears under the synonym *R. sinica Anemone*. In gardens it does best on a warm wall and will in that position go up to a height of 25 feet or more. North of London I have seen it planted in a cold greenhouse (given the sunny wall, and trained up a trellis some 12 feet high, the long growths above that being brought across the roof and over to the other side). The flowers are single, of a rich rose-pink, the largest measuring about 6 inches in diameter. The leaves are composed usually of 3 or 5 leaflets of an attractive glossy green colour. This rose was introduced from Erfurt, Germany, where it originated, towards the end of the last century.

R. banksiae (named in honour of Sir Joseph Banks, commonly known as the Banksian or Banks' Rose). More vigorous than the preceding climber, this rose from China will attain a height of 40 feet in favourable districts. But it does not grow well or bloom in cold, sunless gardens. For this reason the finest specimens are to be found in the South. It is most at home in Italy and the South of France, flowering profusely during April and May. It is a success in Cornwall and Devon, where it is within reach of the warm sea air during the winter months. And in these parts it gives the best show planted on a wall facing south.

There are yellow and white forms, the favourite being the double yellow known as var. *lutea*. It is a pity it is quite scentless. The double white var. *albo-plena* is fragrant. The flowers are numerous and come in clusters, the individual flower measuring about $1\frac{1}{4}$ inches across. They are on stalks about 1 inch long. The leaves, evergreen, with 3 or 5 leaflets, are a pleasing shade of green, which contrasts well with the flowers, yellow or white. This exquisite climbing rose came to us from China in 1796.

R. bracteata (with conspicuous bracts). The Macartney Rose has single white, fragrant flowers (3 to 4 inches across), with golden-yellow stamens, the stalks on which they are carried being surrounded by several large downy bracts. The leaves, usually evergreen, have from 5 to 11 finely-toothed leaflets of a dark, glossy green and are large on vigorous, tall-growing specimens. A fine climbing rose for warm districts, it will go up to a height of 20 feet on a wall.

Grown in a cool greenhouse, as it often is in districts near London, the flowers give off a pleasant fruity smell, not always noticeable on plants out of doors. 'Marie Leonida', with creamy-white double flowers, is one of the garden forms derived from it; 'Mermaid' is the most famous. The species is a native of China and is naturalized in the south-eastern States of North America. It is the only known species wholly immune to Black Spot disease.

R. brunonii (named for the eminent botanist Robert Brown). It is known as the Himalayan Musk Rose and is nearly allied to *R. moschata*. The flowers, single and slightly fragrant, come in large clusters 12 inches in width. Each flower, which opens yellowish and then becomes white, is about 1 inch across. The leaves, deciduous, are an attractive glaucous-green colour. *R. brunonii* is one of the strongest-growing of the wild climbing roses and in its habitat, the Himalayas, ascends tall trees, covering branches 30 feet up with hanging clusters of flowers.

Hillier's catalogue describes it as a rampant climbing species needing full sun and a warm climate. In the garden it is often planted near a holly tree, which it climbs with the help of its stout, hooked thorns.

From *R. eglanteria* are derived the famous Penzance Briars, which have the sweet scent of this native rose. It may be seen full of pale pink flowers in our hedgerows in summer.

The Penzance hybrids grow up to about 10 or 12 feet high and need a pillar or some sort of support to show them off well. Those with a yellowish tinge in their flowers are liked best: 'Lady Penzance' (a delicate copper and yellow colour) is one; 'Lord Penzance' (soft fawn and lemon) is another. The name *Eglantine* is an old English one for the Sweet-briar.

R. filipes. This is another vigorous wild climbing rose. It makes shoots 12 feet long in a season, which carry large clusters of flowers, white tinged with pink and very fragrant. There are from 50 to 80 in a cluster. A plant in full bloom is a lovely sight climbing over old bushes or up a tree. I have seen it used for covering a sunny bank and spreading its stems laden with blossom over the roof of a shed. It is perfectly hardy and thrives in quite poor soils. The individual flowers are 1 inch wide; the dark green leaves have 5 or 7 leaflets, and the small round fruits, which appear in autumn, are bright red. The species is a native of West China. Wilson first discovered it there in 1908.

R. gigantea (giant rose). This is included because it is the most magnificent of all the climbing roses. (There are few districts in this country where it grows and blooms really satisfactorily outside. Some gardeners, however, state that it and its varieties are hardier than most people think.)

The flowers on some wild specimens are said to measure

as much as 12 or 15 inches in diameter – truly, giant flowers, single, fragrant and white or pale yellow and apparently sometimes pink. The leaves, deciduous or evergreen, are large, made up of 5 or 7 leaflets 3 inches long of a glossy green colour. In the wild it sends up its shoots, with thick hooked prickles, 40 feet or more, through shrubs and bushes and reaches the tops of trees. Sir Henry Collett, who discovered the Giant Honeysuckle (*Lonicera hildebrandiana*), introduced this noble rose to Europe in 1889. He found both these climbers in the Shan Hills of Upper Burma. *R. gigantea* was previously discovered in North-eastern India and in Yunnan, China. It was at one time called *R. odorata* var. *gigantea* and thought to be a variety of the Tea Rose. L. H. Bailey, *The Standard Cyclopedia of Horticulture*, says, "*R. odorata gigantea* is hardy only South and is cultivated in California, where it blooms from November to May. Hybrids with *R. moschata* have been raised by Franceschi at Santa Barbara, California; these are 'Madame Lemoine', 'Montarioso', and 'Montecito', and they combine the vigour and the foliage of var. *gigantea* with the paniculate inflorescence of *R. moschata*." (*R. odorata gigantea* is now a synonym.)

The ideal place for this glorious rose, outside a cool greenhouse, is a sunny wall in a warm district. You may see it in full bloom about the beginning of June in the west country along the Atlantic seaboard; and the best and freest-flowering specimens in the warm climates of Italy and the South of France.

It is interesting to hear what Mr. E. A. Bunyard said about the plant 20 years ago. Writing in the R.H.S. Journal on *The Hardiness of Rosa gigantea and its Hybrids*: "Coming from Burma, this rose has been considered tender, but having grown it in the open for many years where it has flowered and seeded I think this opinion should be revised." In our climate it seems that the vigorous shoots are not always ripened off, but when the plant is grown in poor, sandy soil penetrated by the roots of trees, it grows less strongly, the wood ripening and producing shoots which flower. 'La Follette' is a favourite *gigantea* hybrid on the Riviera and succeeds in several gardens south of London. It also flowers well in Gloucestershire, even as early as May. "I think it very probable that 'Gloire de Dijon' [see page 74] has *R. gigantea* blood in its ancestry and this, I learn, is quite hardy in Northumberland, so we may assume that *R. gigantea* itself is not tender in some of its forms."

R. hemisphaerica (referring to the hemispherical shape of the calyx tube). It is a pity one cannot recommend it, for it is one of the loveliest of all the wild roses. Its drooping clusters of very double, sulphur-yellow flowers are exquisite and hang gracefully among the green leaves. But the plant needs more sun than we normally get in this country; even when it grows well on a sheltered wall, it will not flower unless it gets long periods of uninterrupted sunshine. It is so beautiful, it is worth finding a place for it in a cool greenhouse. A native of Western Asia, it was cultivated in the gardens of Persia during the seventh century, and in Britain apparently at the beginning of the seventeenth century. Unfortunately it has never flowered very well here.

In places which suit it, it usually goes up to about 10 feet high on a wall and will bloom in July. The leaflets number 5 to 9 and are a glaucous green; the flowers, 2 inches across, a beautiful sulphur-yellow. Hillier lists this climbing species and describes it, "This rare and beautiful plant from Asia Minor does best when given a warm, sheltered wall. Its wreaths of delicate sulphur-yellow, double flowers, are only freely produced in warm seasons." It needs a light, well-drained soil.

R. laevigata (smooth, polished). This is a native of China and has long been naturalized in the southern United States. It is popularly known as the Cherokee Rose and in Britain is mostly grown on a warm wall, the finest specimens being found in Cornwall and other regions enjoying a mild climate.

Around London it is usually given the protection of a cold greenhouse and under glass goes up to a height of 15 or 20 feet, clinging to the trellis-work, or whatever supports it, with its hooked spines.

One of its great attractions is its leathery evergreen leaves; they are 3-foliolate, brilliantly glossy and quite small. On trellis in a greenhouse, the foliage affords a good background to any other plants that come into flower during the winter months. The flowers are white, solitary, about 4 inches across and sweetly-scented.

It is not known when the plant reached the U.S.A., but it was cultivated in Georgia in 1780. Specimens were collected in that

State (escapes from gardens) some 20 years later by the American botanist Pursh.

Most shrub specialists stock the plant.

There is a well-known hybrid climber derived from it called 'Anemone', which has large, single, pink flowers shaded with rose. It may be slightly hardier than the species itself, though it flowers more freely and grows strongest on a warm wall.

R. multiflora (many flowered) is one of the parents of the much-loved *polyantha* roses, which are so popular today with gardeners.

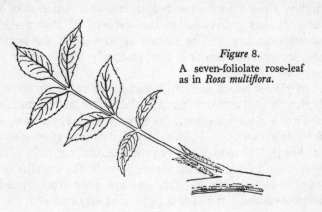

Figure 8.
A seven-foliolate rose-leaf as in *Rosa multiflora.*

The species is native to Northern China, Korea and Japan where it makes a tall, bushy plant 10 feet or more high. In gardens it is usually trained up trellis-work or up stout supports. The flowers, fragrant, are white or flesh-pink, 1 inch wide, with golden-yellow stamens, and come in large, branching panicles. The leaves have 7 or 9 leaflets varying from 1 to 2 inches long; the fruits or heps are small and red, oval to round in shape and bright and decorative in the autumn.

In its habitat it is found rambling through tall shrubs and climbing trees 20 feet or more in height; and it can be allowed to grow in this way under cultivation. Planted in conjunction with *R. filipes*, both climbing up some sparsely-branched tree, such as a Laburnum, a wonderfully rich effect of pink and white blossom will be had in midsummer.

The variety *platyphylla* (broad-leaved), known as the 'Seven Sisters Rose', has broader leaves and very double, large, purplish flowers varying from pale to deep crimson-purple. The popular name originated apparently from the different shades of colour.

R. setigera (bristle-bearing). The species is commonly known as the Prairie Rose and although it has little or no fragrance, it is a valuable climber, since it is probably the last of the wild rambling roses to bloom. Completely hardy and free-flowering, and one of the strongest-growing in cultivation. It often makes shoots as much as 15 feet in a season. The flowers, which come in clusters, are about 2 inches wide, rose-coloured at first, then fading to white; the leaflets, 3 or 5, are sharply-toothed.

The species is native to eastern and central North America and is found as far south as Florida. It is most at home rambling over shrubs (of no ornamental value); but it is also used as a pergola rose.

It deserves to be more widely grown as do the hybrids derived from it. 'Baltimore Belle' and 'Queen of the Prairies' are two: both have double flowers.

R. wichuraiana (named in honour of Max E. Wichura, one of the botanists on the German expedition to China and Japan in 1859–61). A semi-evergreen trailing rose from Asia, making shoots 15 or 20 feet long in a season. It is mostly used for covering sunny banks, and there looks perhaps best. Old tree stumps make good supports and show off well the clusters of white fragrant flowers and glossy green leaves. It is grown too in large rockeries, where its flowers are particularly welcome in August among the faded alpine plants. The individual flowers are about 2 inches across and come in panicles; the leaves usually have 7 or 9 leaflets.

R. wichuraiana was introduced to Kew from North America in 1891. The plant is one of the parents of our most popular garden ramblers.

Hillier lists the species and describes it as "Most suitable for covering banks, tree-stumps, etc. Leaves small, lustrous; flowers small, white, richly-scented."

These wild climbing roses are not widely grown in our gardens; no doubt the more showy garden forms have become the established favourites; but they lack the individuality of the wild plants and often need richer, well-fed soils. The species can be left unpruned when they are grown on trees and planted in any ordinary garden soil, which will need no manuring.

The best method of propagating these wild kinds for the average gardener is by cuttings, which should be taken about August and inserted in sandy soil in a frame. They will often root out of doors, however, if they are taken in July and covered with a bell-glass.

The hybrid ramblers and climbers are bewilderingly numerous; and the owner of a small garden confronted with a list of several hundred may decide it would be best for a nursery to choose one for him. It is a good idea. It would be wise, too, to visit the nursery and see a selection of plants in bloom. Some varieties do better in one position than another. 'Albertine', for instance, is often a failure on a sunny wall. It is one of the Wichuraiana group of climbers, which prefer an open position in the garden to a wall, where more often than not they contract some sort of disease. The following, obtainable from most nurseries, are some of the best.

'Albéric Barbier.' A small-flowered, very popular Climber. The parents are *R. wichuraiana* × 'Shirley Hibberd'. Creamy-white, semi-double flowers, rich yellow in the bud. The small, glossy green leaves are a great attraction. It can be trained on a trellis (not against a wall) or up the supports of a pergola, or left alone, several in a row, to form a tall screen. Raised by Barbier in 1900.

'Albertine.' Another climber from the same nursery; raised in 1909. Its parentage is *R. wichuraiana* × 'Mrs. A. R. Wadell'. Almost as well known as the preceding. Grown together over an arbour or up a pergola, they produce a glorious effect. Both need drastic pruning the first year they are planted to encourage basal growth. Then, apart from the removal of the old wood, they need little attention. The flowers are carried on the new growths.

'Allen Chandler' is a Hybrid Climbing Tea, a 'Hugh Dickson' seedling. It was raised by Chandler in 1923 and is one of the finest of the rich red climbers. The flowers are large and look very striking against a grey stone wall. The plant is moderately vigorous and needs a good rich soil. No pruning is necessary till it is well established. The Hybrid Climbing Tea Roses are best treated in this way.

'American Pillar.' A *Wichuraiana* rambler. It has single, deep pink flowers with a white centre; they come in large clusters in late June. The plant is very vigorous and is often used for pergolas. It flowers in late June and needs moderate pruning. Its parentage is *R. wichuraiana* × (*R. setigera*, the Prairie Rose) × a red hybrid perpetual.

I would like to mention 'Adélaide d'Orléans', an old rose from the evergreen *R. sempervirens*. It was raised by M. Jacques, who was gardener to the Duke of Orleans, and introduced in 1829. It is very similar in colour to 'Félicité et Perpétue' (blush-pink fading to white), another climber from the same species. The flowers are loosely formed and hang downwards and look particularly charming on a pergola. Unfortunately I have been unable to get a specimen from any nursery.

'Chaplin's Pink Climber' is of the same class as 'American Pillar' and should be similarly treated. The flowers, semi-double, soft pink with golden-yellow stamens, last well into the autumn. It is a good rose for pillars and arches. I have seen it trained up tall massive poles set up in two rows forming a sort of avenue. The method is rather formal and does not appeal to everybody.

There are many climbing forms of the popular hybrid varieties: any rose list contains a goodish number. Some unfortunately do not bloom freely and seem hardly worth the room they take up. The following, however, a small selection, have proved good flowerers on walls, trellis and the like.

'Climbing Lady Hillingdon.' (Hicks, 1927.) This is one of the loveliest of the yellow roses for a warm south or a west wall. (The colour is a bright buff-yellow.) The flowers come on long, slender shoots and in the bud are of an orange-yellow shade. It does not give a second show of flowers as do many of the climbers here described.

'Climbing Madame Caroline Testout' is a sport of the Hybrid Tea, with large bright pink fragrant flowers – a well-known rose. It gives a good display of blooms during the early summer and a moderately good one later. Excellent for a sunny wall.

'Climbing Ophelia.' Another Hybrid Tea sport and as popular as the preceding one. Salmon-pink coloured blooms of a beautiful shape. I have found that it does as well on a west wall as anywhere. It is trained sometimes on a pergola; it gives a moderate second show in the autumn.

'Climbing Peace' has pale yellow blooms, delicately edged with pink. A very sweet-smelling rose; a vigorous climber.

'Climbing Princess Marina' has apricot flowers heavily veined and shaded salmon; they are fragrant and of good shape. An excellent climber for a pillar.

These climbing sports must not be cut back at all the first year they are planted; and on the whole they need very little pruning: dead wood and overcrowded growths are cut out and the lateral shoots shortened according to their vigour. A good rich loam is required, neither too acid nor too limy. A heavy texture is recommended by many rose-growers.

'Crimson Conquest.' A Wichuraiana Climber, which has smallish semi-double bright crimson flowers, with yellow stamens. The flowers are freely carried during the summer, but there is no later show. It is recommended for training on a pergola and looks better there, I think, than on a wall, where its faded flowers are more conspicuous. As it flowers on the lateral shoots as well as on the growths made the previous year, it requires a moderate pruning.

'Crimson Shower.' A Wichuraiana Rambler which, like others similar to it ('Dorothy Perkins', for instance) needs pruning after it has finished flowering, the old wood being cut out and the new growths, which will bloom, trained up in their place. It is a seedling from 'Excelsa' (see page 73), a vigorous rambler, with semi-double crimson flowers which bloom from July to mid-September. It was raised by Messrs. Norman in 1951.

'Cupid' is a vigorous climber with large leaves and large single flowers, bright pink shaded yellow. It does well on a warm wall in most districts and blooms only during the summer. It needs little pruning apart from cutting out unwanted wood.

'Dr. W. Van Fleet' was raised by Van Fleet in 1910. It has flesh-pink, fragrant flowers, large and double, and is a vigorous rambler which can be used in several ways: on pergolas, trellis (for screening) and, best of all, allowed to climb freely up old trees. Pruning is the same as for 'Albertine' and 'Albéric Barbier'.

'Dorothy Perkins': the old favourite rambler: perhaps the

best known of all the garden climbing roses. It was raised by Jackson and Perkins in 1901; its parents are *R. wichuraiana* × 'Mme Gabriel Luizet'. The small, full, pink flowers are well known and are best displayed on a pergola. The plant needs plenty of room and should be given a place where it can grow freely. It is not suitable for walls, where it will often contract mildew as it does in a cold, draughty situation. It flowers on the new, vigorous growths. It only needs the old wood cutting out. The foliage is almost evergreen.

'Easlea's Golden Rambler.' A strong-growing Wichuraiana Climber with yellow flowers splashed with crimson. The olive-green foliage contrasts well with the flowers and is attractive before they open. A good rambler for a pillar. Pruning the same as for 'Albertine'.

'Emily Grey' seldom gives a good show till it is well established. Then it requires little or no pruning. It was raised by Williams in 1918; the parentage is 'Jersey Beauty' × 'Comtesse du Cayla'. The flowers are golden-yellow, large and fragrant; the foliage is a charming glossy green touched with bronze.

'Evangeline.' A vigorous rambler belonging to the 'Dorothy Perkins' class. It is a popular rose for covering tall trellis-work, where its single, fragrant pale pink flowers, which come on long sprays, are displayed to advantage. It is at its best in July. Its parents are *R. wichuraiana* × 'Crimson Rambler'.

'Excelsa.' A bright crimson 'Dorothy Perkins'. Introduced 50 years ago, it is still one of the best ramblers. The flowers are double and come in late summer. A strong-growing plant often used for training as a Weeping Rose.

'Félicité et Perpétué' like 'Adélaide d'Orléans' is a seedling of *R. sempervirens*. It retains its foliage well into the winter and is thus a valuable rambler for a wall or for training over an arbour. The flowers, a blush-pink fading to white, are exquisitely formed, the smaller central petals lying back neatly on the larger ones. It was raised by M. Jacques in 1827 and named after the two Carthaginian Martyrs, St. Félicitas and St. Perpetua. It is often grown on a tree or a tall shrub, but slender-branched plants such as *Buddleia davidii* are not strong enough for it. It needs tough, strong branches to support the wonderful mass of flowers. Only a light pruning is necessary.

'François Juranville'. (*R. wichuraiana* × 'Mme Laurette

Messimy'.) An early bloomer. The double, pink flowers, shaded copper, are deliciously fragrant. An excellent rose for a screen, but does not bloom freely unless the stems are cut back every second or third year.

'Gloire de Dijon' should be pruned like the Climbing Sports described. It was raised by Jacotot in 1852 and is known to every rose-lover. The buff-yellow flowers come freely on good specimens such as one sees in old-world gardens. It is best on a south or a west wall.

'Hiawatha.' Raised in 1904 by Messrs. Walsh. ('Crimson Rambler' × 'Paul's Carmine Pillar'). This Wichuraiana Rambler has small, single, crimson flowers with a white centre and yellow stamens. The flowers come in large clusters and show up well against the glossy green foliage. It is a vigorous grower, suitable for an archway or for a pergola. Only the old wood should be cut out.

'High Noon.' A Climbing Hybrid Tea with yellow flowers and golden stamens. Its upright growth makes it suitable for a pillar. It is often seen trained up a pergola. A long blooming season.

'Lady Gay' is preferred by many gardeners to 'Dorothy Perkins' because it is less susceptible to mildew. It is similar to that plant and one of the Wichuraiana ramblers. It has small, deep rose-pink flowers and glossy green foliage. Cut out the old wood.

'Lady Godiva.' Another rambler of the same group. Pale blush-pink flowers come on long, slender shoots and in the bud are of an orange-yellow shade.

'Lady Waterlow.' A climbing Hybrid Tea with semi-double salmon and deep pink flowers – large and full. Excellent for a wall. Little pruning: remove only the dead wood.

'Lemon Pillar.' A pale lemon-yellow rose. The flowers are large, full and very fragrant and carried in profusion. I have seen it grown on pergolas, on fences, and rambling over tall shrubs. It is a Climbing Hybrid Tea and needs little pruning.

'Léontine Gervais.' (*R. wichuraiana* × 'Souvenir de Catherine Guillot'.) Large, double blooms, salmon-pink, slightly fragrant; the foliage is glossy green, an excellent foil to the flowers. A June-flowering rose, which is particularly lovely on an arch.

'Maréchal Niel' is a seedling of *R. noisettiana* which is a cross between an *R. chinensis* hybrid and *R. brunonii*. It is one of many fine seedlings, none of which is particularly hardy. 'Maréchal Niel', raised in 1886, is often grown under glass; it does well on a warm wall in the South and there will carry large, very fragrant, pale golden-yellow flowers. It needs little pruning. None the first year.

'Marjorie Foster.' A Wichuraiana Rambler of moderate growth. It has large clusters of cup-shaped, double flowers, crimson-scarlet.

'Mary Hicks.' Another moderately-vigorous rambler. Scarlet flowers. Lovely on a pillar.

'Mary Wallace.' A summer-flowering semi-double rose-pink rambler, often used for pergolas or for a tall wooden trellis screen. Not good on a wall. Its parentage is R. *wichuraiana* ✕ a Hybrid Tea.

'Mermaid' is an R. *bracteata* seedling and one of the loveliest of our climbers (see page 64). It was raised by Paul in 1918. On a warm wall it attains a height of 20 or 30 feet and blooms till the frosts come. The slightly-fragrant, single, large flowers (often 6 inches across) are primrose-yellow, with amber-coloured stamens, and begin to open at the end of June. The glossy, green foliage, almost evergreen in mild districts, is bronzy-red in its young state and appears to be immune to mildew. This climber is best left to grow freely and not pruned. Unfortunately, its young wood is brittle, the new branches being easily snapped off from the main stems.

'Minnehaha.' (R. *wichuraiana* ✕ 'Paul Neyron'.) The small, deep pink flowers, rosette-shaped, come in large, loose panicles; they are slightly fragrant and at their best in July. It is mostly used on a pergola. The new wood produces the flowers.

'Paul's Scarlet Climber.' A Wichuraiana Climber with intense scarlet, smallish, semi-double flowers. It is especially decorative on a pergola; the stems, with their clusters of hanging flowers, should be trained across the roofing beams.

'Phyllis Bide' is a moderately-tall rambler, with pinkish-yellow flowers, which is most suitable for a pillar. It goes up to a height of 6 feet or so. Only the dead and exhausted wood should be removed. It does not need pruning the first year.

'Purity.' A pure white, semi-double, climbing rose, with rich glossy foliage. It is often seen on pergolas; and is most effective when it is allowed to climb up through tall shrubs, which it ascends with the help of its stout, hooked thorns. It blooms in early summer and is one of the best white-flowered climbers. Once established, it needs very little pruning. Its parentage is *R. wichuraiana* × 'Mme Caroline Testout'. It was raised by Hooper in 1917.

'Record' is a bright scarlet climber, with large, semi-double flowers. ('Paul's Scarlet Climber' × 'Demain'.) A moderately-tall pillar rose which blooms very freely in summer.

'Sander's White.' A Wichuraiana Rambler which is often used for training over arches or on pergolas. It is not always a success on a wall. The pure white flowers, which are slightly fragrant, come in early summer.

'Snow Flake' is another pure white rambler of the same class. A vigorous climber for a pergola or a stout wooden trellis screen. The flowers are fragrant and at their best in midsummer.

'Tausendschön.' Raised by Schmidt in 1906. A 'Crimson, Rambler' seedling. It has rose-pink, slightly fragrant flowers, which are freely carried in summer. Unfortunately, it mildews badly.

'Thelma.' (*R. wichuraiana* × 'Paul's Scarlet Climber'.) A soft, pale pink colour, the semi-double flowers showing up well on a pillar. The plant seldom goes above 6 or 7 feet in height.

'The New Dawn.' Another Wichuraiana Rambler. It is a sport from 'Dr. Van Fleet', and has fragrant, double shell-pink flowers. Moderately vigorous and excellent for a pillar.

'Veilchenblau' (Violet-blue). Raised by Schmidt in 1909. A hybrid of *R. multiflora*. The colour is crimson passing to violet, the flowers coming in large clusters. The plant will reach a height of 20 feet or more on a shady wall and bloom freely during the summer.

'Zéphirine Drouhin.' A Hybrid Bourbon rose raised by Bizet in 1868. It has large, bright pink, semi-double fragrant flowers, which come in the summer; often blooms will be seen on the plant at Christmas. It is a moderately-vigorous climbing rose (thornless), suitable for walls, fences or pillars. The wood only needs thinning occasionally.

The Australian Climbing Roses are becoming more popular and are among the most beautiful of our garden roses. They were raised by an Australian grower and are offered for sale by various rose nurseries. Three of the best known are:

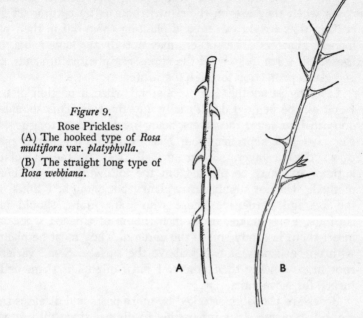

Figure 9.
Rose Prickles:
(A) The hooked type of *Rosa multiflora* var. *platyphylla*.
(B) The straight long type of *Rosa webbiana*.

A   B

'Black Boy', which has large, semi-double flowers shaded with blackish-crimson. A remarkably-rich colour.

'Gwen Nash' is valuable for its long-blooming season (most of the summer to the autumn) and has flowers 6 inches across, semi-double, with large petals, a cyclamen-pink paling toward the centre.

'Queen of Hearts' has semi-double, rich rose-pink flowers the same size. Both of these roses have a conspicuous centre of yellow stamens, which add much to their charm. The flowers come in profusion during the summer months.

A new race of ramblers is the *Kordesii*. The plants are covered with blooms from top to bottom (most effective adorning a pillar) and they bloom continuously from the summer to late autumn. Two I recommend are:

'Hamburger Phoenix', with long sprays of semi-double, crimson flowers which have a faint smell of musk. A strong growing plant.

'Leverkusen' has golden-yellow flowers and is a good strong rambler for training over an arch or on a pergola.

77

The easiest method of propagating the garden climbing roses when they are on their own roots is by cutting off any suckers that are thrown up and planting them out in their permanent quarters. The suckers may not always have roots, but these will form quickly, if the stems are planted in sandy soil and given protection through the winter.

Layering is another simple method when a portion of firm wood can be pegged down easily into the soil. This should be done in late June, the layers being made with a tongue (see Fig. 10) and kept firmly in place with a fork-shaped piece of wood. The layers should normally root by the end of the autumn and may be planted out the following spring. These methods will not supply many plants, but enough, I think, for the average gardener. Those who want more, should take cuttings. For outside, use 6-inch shoots of ripened wood and insert them in sandy soil in the autumn. They must be planted with one eye only showing above the surface. Some varieties root more quickly than others. I have often left them undisturbed for 12 months.

Roses are probably attacked by more pests and diseases than any other plants. It is impossible to discuss them fully in this limited space. Many pests can be destroyed by Nicotine-Soap Wash or by Nicotine Dust. As regards diseases: Black Spot and Powdery Mildew are two of the most prevalent. The leaves affected with the former should be picked off and burned. And it may be combated by spraying with Bordeaux Mixture from

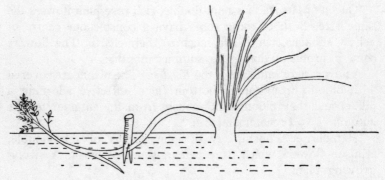

Figure 10.

A method of layering a rose by 'tonguing' or splitting the buried stem.

June onwards. The same mixture is also used for Powdery Mildew.

When climbing roses are grown on walls, it is necessary to support the plants by some means or other: trellis-work is best, or wires may be used. Those that are suitable for climbing up trees and over shrubs will make their way through the upper branches with the help of their thorns.

[5]

THE VIRGINIA CREEPER (*Vitis quinquefolia*) is the most popular of the climbers we grow for their brilliantly-coloured autumn foliage. It is as easy and as vigorous as the Ivy, doing well in any ordinary garden soil and in practically any place where it is planted. It is said to colour best on walls, especially those facing south or west; though I have seen it give a magnificent display on trees of great height, which it has ascended.

Some botanists refer to it as a Vine and give it the specific name mentioned above. The plant appears under this name in Bean's *Trees and Shrubs Hardy in the British Isles* (Ed. 1951). *Parthenocissus* is the group in the *Genus Vitis*, in which it is included (that Group comprising some ten species). It is now regarded by many botanists as a separate genus; and the Virginia Creeper appears as *Parthenocissus quinquefolia*. Other names under which it has been described are *Ampelopsis quinquefolia* and *Vitis hederacea*; these are now synonyms.

The name comes from the Greek *parthenos*, virgin; *kissos*, Ivy. The French call the plant *vigne* (vine), *vierge* (virgin). Parkinson (1629) speaks of it, "This slender, but tall climbing Virginia Vine (as it was first called; but *Ivie*, as it doth better resemble)."

For a display of autumnal colour there are few hardy climbers to beat it. (Other species included by botanists in *Parthenocissus* are described in Chapter three under *Vitis*.)

The specific epithet *quinquefolia* refers to the leaves, which are composed of mostly 5 leaflets measuring from 1 to 4 inches long. These are coarsely-toothed except near the base; dull

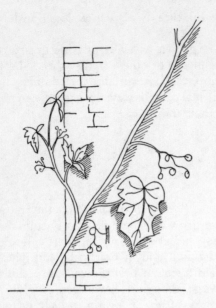

Figure 11.

Type of branched-tendril which forms adhesive discs; these becoming cemented to the surface (as in virginia creeper).

green above, paler and rather glaucous beneath. The fruits, blue-black, round and about $\frac{1}{4}$ inch in diameter, only ripen after a particularly hot summer. The tendrils are branched and provided with discs, with which the plant clings to any surface. It is therefore most useful for covering walls, fences and the trunks of trees.

When planted on buildings, it should be kept from reaching the eaves and from encroaching on any important architectural details. For many years the noble pilastered structure of the main façade of Clare College Chapel, Cambridge, was completely hidden by a thick mass of it; fortunately it has now been removed. The leaves which come on the lower branches of the creeper are much larger and coarser than those on the higher stems.

Climbers like the Virginia Creeper which adhere to surfaces by means of disc-tipped tendrils require, of course, no support as do some of the twiners. The tendrils of this plant turn naturally away from the light, toward the wall or the surface, to which they will adhere – they are referred to by some botanists as 'light-avoiding tendrils'. (See also page 171.) The leaves, on the other hand, in search of light and air, extend outwards. When the tendril-branches touch the surface, they begin to spread out, thicken and form discs which become cemented to it, so strongly in fact that it is impossible to detach them. When repeated efforts are made to pull the creeper off any surface, the tendrils are torn away from the discs, which are permanently attached to it. Fig. 11, page 80 shows this type of branching-tendril. (See *Vitis vitacea*, Chapter 3, page 175 for another type of branched-tendril; the thread-like ends twining round twigs and stems.)

The Virginia Creeper, sometimes called the True Virginia Creeper, is a native of North America and was introduced into Britain about 1629. But until some years back it had actually become rather rare in cultivation, another species called Virginia Creeper (*Vitis vitacea*) being widely grown in our gardens. This plant, however, has no adhesive discs and is therefore unable to cling to any surface. It supports itself by twining its tendrils round twigs and branches as do many of the Vines – the edible Grape, for instance. Its use in the garden is consequently more limited; but its autumn tints are as beautiful as those of the genuine Virginia Creeper.

At Kew Botanic Gardens the latter plant climbs up tall pines and gives a glorious show of scarlet in November.

Vitis quinquefolia is easily raised from hardwood cuttings or by layers.

[6]

WISTARIA is the last of our popular families of ornamental climbers to be described. It is less often seen perhaps than Clematis, Jasmine, Honeysuckle and Roses; many gardeners, I believe, suspect it might be difficult to grow. It often fails to bloom if it is not planted in the right place and is not pruned correctly.

The genus was named in honour of the anatomist Caspar Wistar (1761–1818) of Pennsylvania. The name sometimes appears as WISTERIA and is spelt this way in botanical works.

It is a small genus, consisting of 7 species: deciduous climbing twiners: 2 from N. America; the others from Japan or China.

F

Wistaria sinensis (Chinese) is by far the most popular kind and is almost exclusively grown in our gardens. In *Curtis's Botanical Magazine* (Vol. 46), 1819, it is described as being brought from China in 1816 by Captain Welbank (the plant was found growing in a garden in Canton), and it was kept in that gentleman's peach-house, heated to 84° F., "where it was nearly destroyed by the red spider". This first specimen seemed to have endured a great deal but it survived and flourished. "On the heat being reduced to below 60° F., the plant was more vigorous, but still weakly. Early in August the gardener removed it from the wall of the peach-house, set it in a pot of vegetable mould, and tied the branches to a stake. In the middle of September it lost all its leaves. . . ."

The species is a native of Northern China and in the course of years makes a woody, twining climber up to 100 feet tall in the warmer parts of the world. The trunks of old specimens are often 5 feet or more in circumference and although hollowed by the ravages of time and disease continue to produce strong, healthy stems laden with flowers.

It is the noblest of all the hardy, woody climbing plants for a wall and needs supports for the young sappy growths. When these mature, they are firm enough to support themselves. In fact this *Wistaria* is trained in many gardens to form a bush- or tree-like plant. It is pruned back regularly to a height of about 6 feet for some years; it then forms a thick, main woody trunk and the top spreads out, forming a bushy head.

The leaves are usually made up of about 11 leaflets which are 1 inch to 3 inches long; the flowers, pea-shaped, lavender mauve, come in long pendulous racemes. They are carried on growths made during the previous season, the young stems being covered with silky down.

W. sinensis is usually at its best in May and earlier than that in the South of France and Italy, where, outside its habitat, the finest specimens may be seen. (It is not a great success in the Midlands and the north of England unless it is given a warm, sunny wall.) Claude Monet grew a magnificent plant in his garden at Giverny (Southern France), the village where he settled to paint. It was trained over the bridge which spanned the lake where he grew his famous water-lilies. No doubt its long roots reached the moist loam near the water and kept the plant well fed during the hot summer months. Sun it must have on its flowering stems, and in the South of France it gets all it needs.

The popular way of growing it in Japan is to train it under the eaves all round the house – the houses are low buildings. By careful, annual pruning, the long racemes, in two or more rows, hang down the walls, and the leaves are above.

If it is grown on a wall, it must be one facing due south which is in the sun practically all day long. It doesn't seem to do so well on a west wall.

As regards pruning: this should be done in winter, the stems being cut back to within a few inches of the old wood to form strong flowering spurs. It is important to keep those Wistarias trained on a wall regularly pruned otherwise they make a lot of growth which seldom produces much blossom. The ends of the stems often carry a few flowers in August and September. Cut them off as soon as the flowers have faded; then prune back hard in December.

There are several varieties of *W. sinensis*: the best known is the white-flowered *W. sinensis* var. *alba*.

The other species are not so widely grown in this country (apart, perhaps, from *W. floribunda* var. *macrobotrys*), but as there are so few, we will describe them here.

W. floribunda (abounding in flowers). Commonly known as the Japanese Wistaria and native to Japan, where, according to L. H. Bailey, "it is common on the margins of woods and along streams". Other writers regard it as rather rare in the wild but very common in cultivation; it is often seen in temple gardens.

It reaches a height of 30 feet or more and has dark, glossy green leaves composed of 11 to 19 leaflets and fragrant purplish-blue flowers in racemes from 5 to 10 inches long, the individual flowers opening successively from the base.

The species was introduced into Belgium from Japan by the eminent botanist Siebold in 1830.

It is less often seen in our gardens than the variety *W. floribunda macrobotrys* (with large, long clusters), which is favoured for the length of its racemes. In some gardens in Japan these are said to be between 5 and 6 feet along. They are wonderfully displayed by an ancient plant growing on a bridge at Kameido.

It carries thousands of racemes in the summer which attract visitors from many parts of the world.

Because of the length of its racemes, it is more effective on a structure where they can hang freely: a pergola, for example, or the stems can be trained over the criss-cross rafters roofing an arbour or a summer-house.

The plant has been described as a variety of *W. sinensis* by some botanists, but it is quite distinct: the racemes are longer, the leaves have more leaflets, and it blooms some weeks later.

There are several other varieties, viz. var. *alba*, with white flowers tinged with lilac; var. *rosea* has pale rose flowers tipped with purple; var. *russelliana*, which has flowers darker than those of the type (the last was named for John Russell, Richmond, Surrey).

W. × *formosa* (beautiful) is a hybrid between *W. sinensis* and *W. floribunda* var. *alba* and considered by many growers to be more beautiful than its parents. I do not know whether it is obtainable from nurseries nowadays – some years back it was impossible to get a specimen. Its flowers are pale violet, opening almost simultaneously, carried in racemes about 10 inches long. The leaves are downy at first, then bright green and smooth on the upper surface. This Wistaria was raised in the garden of Professor C. S. Sargent at Holm Lea, Brookline, Massachusetts, in 1905 and introduced to Kew about 1920.

W. frutescens (shrubby). The species is figured in *Curtis's Botanical Magazine* (Vol. 46), 1819, where the flower (raceme) appears rather like a Lupin. (The dull, inky mauve colour does not tempt one to buy a specimen.) The plant is less showy than the two kinds most widely grown, viz. *W. sinensis* and *W. floribunda* var. *macrobotrys*. It does better, too, in warm southern countries than it does with us. The author of the article in the *Botanical Magazine* says, "A very ornamental shrub, tolerably hardy, but does not flower very readily except in favourable situations. There used to be a very fine plant trained up against the house at Messrs. Loddiges & Sons at Hackney; which, in some years, bore a profusion of flowers. Our drawing was taken from a specimen communicated in June last by Thomas Wildman, Esq., late of Layton.

"Grows naturally in the swamps of Virginia, Carolina, and the Illinois. Introduced in 1724 by Mr. Mark Catesby."

It was the first of the Wistarias to be grown in Britain. No doubt the introduction of superior kinds – *W. sinensis* (1816), for instance – caused it to be less frequently cultivated. .

It is a tall, spreading climber, with twining stems, reaching a height of 30 or 40 feet in nature. The leaves have from 9 to 15 leaflets; the flowers, terminal racemes, are from 4 to 6 inches long and very downy and bloom from the end of June to the end of August. The species is not listed in any current catalogues I have consulted.

W. japonica (Japanese). Like the above species it is not well known here. It is well adapted to growing on trees and is a charming picture covering the branches of an old apple-tree. It deserves to be grown for its late flowers; these are pale yellow or white and come in racemes from 6 to 12 inches long. A native of Japan, this Wistaria was introduced for Messrs. Veitch by Maries in 1878 and flowered for the first time in August, 1884. The species has been placed in the genus *Milletti* by some botanists.

W. macrostachys (with large or long panicles). It is rare in gardens and, like *W. frutescens*, a native of the U.S.A. It grows up trees and reaches a height of 20 or 30 feet. It has racemes of mauvish flowers. The plant was cultivated under the name of *W. frutescens magnifica* in the U.S.A. It is very similar to *W. frutescens*; the chief differences are the larger racemes and the rather larger leaves.

W. venusta (lovely, graceful). This species is offered for sale by several nurseries: Marchant's listed it as "A rare and beautiful climber, producing in quantity, short stocky racemes of large, white, deliciously-scented flowers. These are borne in May and June." It is sometimes called the Silky Wistaria on account of its stems and foliage being covered with soft down. The hanging racemes of white, scented flowers are from 4 to 6 inches long and come in profusion in late May and June. The leaves are composed of usually 11 leaflets, ovalish in shape, the undersides being especially downy.

This lovely climber was first introduced into England in May, 1912 but is not often seen in our gardens. It is perfectly hardy and looks particularly lovely grown as a companion to the common lavender-mauve *W. sinensis*.

W. venusta is not known in the wild, the original plants

coming from Japanese gardens, where it is a favourite climber. A violet-flowered form, however, was found growing on the hills near Nagasaki on the island of Kyushu by Richard Oldham in 1863. It was named *W. venusta* var. *violacea* by Dr. Rehder and is the wild type. There is a double-flowered white form called var. *plena*, which is supposed to have been in cultivation in Britain some years before the single.

Wistarias are among the most beautiful of the woody climbing plants that can be grown in this country. They thrive and flower more freely in our southern counties than they do in the north. If they are grown in exposed gardens which get a lot of wind, they should be trained up a south wall. It won't be wise to grow them on trees in the open.

In warm, sunny gardens they flourish and bloom profusely and are often planted against an old tree. The stems need some support till they are long enough to twine themselves round the branches. A method used by many gardeners is to start the plants off in a bottomless tub, filled with good, rich loam, which is sunk in the ground. This is an excellent idea and necessary, I think, when the plant is to be trained up a tree whose spreading, fibrous roots have impoverished the soil. And it will be necessary also to lop off some of the branches to enable the sun to get to the flowering stems of the climber. A dead tree, denuded of its foliage and therefore able to let in plenty of sun, is of course most suitable.

A favourite tree is the Laburnum, whose hanging racemes of lemon-yellow flowers are similar in shape to those of the common Wistaria. The plants bloom at the same time and the lavender-mauve and the yellow blend delightfully.

When grown on trees, Wistarias need no pruning; they are best left alone to make as much wood as possible. On walls and pergolas, they should be pruned back hard in the winter. The flower-buds are formed at the base of the stems.

Wistarias do not transplant well; they suffer a severe check after they have been moved and large specimens sometimes do not recover.

The plants are usually propagated by layering the stems in summer; they are left for a year, then cut off and planted in their permanent quarters.

These half a dozen families of climbers, *Clematis, Jasminum,*

Lonicera, Rosa, Vitis and *Wistaria*, are the most popular in this country and they provide a large enough choice for most gardeners.

There are several, such as *Jasminum polyanthum* (page 44), which everybody would like to grow, but are too tender for many gardens. They can be planted in pots, where space is limited, or in tubs, where a cool greenhouse is available. The potted specimens are easily moved outside during the summer months; the tubbed plants, if grown in a well-ventilated greenhouse, will thrive and flower well. In the following chapter various kinds suitable for pots or tubs are described including some which cannot be grown permanently out of doors in these islands.

CHAPTER TWO

Climbers and Trailers for Pots and Tubs

MANY of the plants listed here may be seen growing in cool greenhouses; where there is room they are best planted in specially made-up beds of loam and will flourish there, as they will have a good root-run. In pots they may need a move occasionally – if the soil becomes exhausted. But many can be left undisturbed for years and will give a fine show of flowers or foliage. The tender Canary Island Ivy, for example, with its leaves variegated green and creamy-yellow, will thrive for a long time in a 6-inch pot; the plant is supported by a rod about 18 inches tall and mostly kept to that height. There are plenty of other climbers that can be similarly cultivated and used for indoor decoration.

People who live in towns and have no gardens will be specially interested in this method of growing plants.

Whether they are housed in living-rooms or in a greenhouse, it is essential to choose the right type of receptacle. For a young specimen of the Canary Island Ivy, only a small pot is needed. (Nurseries send their Ivies out in pots: they are then left undisturbed, for the right soil will have been prepared for them.) In a big, 12-inch pot the single stem of leaves would look out of place; and in a tub (twice the size) rather absurd.

Different types of receptacles can be bought from nurseries or from local stores; they will be clean and ready for use. Tubs

88

or similar containers not specially designed to hold plants, must be thoroughly scrubbed and have drainage-holes bored in them. I prefer to stand tubs on wooden blocks to prevent surplus moisture collecting underneath.

The potting-medium depends first on the type of climber to be grown. The lime and chalk present in some composts would not be suitable for, say, the tender *Lapageria rosea,* which needs a peaty, loamy, lime-free soil. But many will succeed in a good, sandy loam: it can be bought from a horticultural sundriesman. The John Innes Composts are well known.

The soil should be richer than that used for the same climber out of doors and, when filling up, it should come to within about $\frac{1}{2}$ inch of the top of the pot, the space left enabling the plant to be watered more easily.

Gardeners who cultivate plants in tubs in a greenhouse often fix a zinc ring about 4 inches wide round the inside rim and fill this false top with a rich loam; a method they resort to when re-potting has to be delayed for a season or two.

Drainage is provided by putting a quantity of broken crocks or rubble at the bottom of the receptacle.

In pots the climbers can be supported by a bamboo cane or twigs, or trained over some sort of trellis-work shaped to show off the flowers to best advantage. The tender *Allamandas* (from Tropical America) are sometimes trained over a balloon-shaped trellis fixed in a large pot. And where there is a heated greenhouse, some of the tallest varieties give a magnificent show on wires running up the wall and across the roof.

Many climbers on the tender side will be all right grown in tubs on a veranda. They may need some protection during a severe winter – materials such as polythene covers are admirable for the purpose.

Annual climbing plants like the *Ipomoea* (*I. purpurea* or *Pharbitis purpurea* is a special favourite) are often grown in pots for indoor decoration and easily raised from seed.

Cucurbita (Ornamental Gourds) is another genus, but not so frequently seen as the *Ipomoea.* Species and varieties of both these genera, along with other annual climbers, are included in the following descriptive list.

The first, *Allamanda,* needs a heated greenhouse, the temperature of which should never be below 55° F. Not many people, then, will be able to grow these exotics: yet I have seen some varieties growing and flowering well in a large pot in a living-room.

The genus was named to commemorate Dr. Allamand of Leyden, who sent seed of a species to the famous botanist Linnaeus.

Where room can be found for the plants in a heated greenhouse, the stems should be tied to wires (I have also seen lengths of plastic clothes-line used). Their flowers are mostly bright yellow, funnel-shaped, with spreading lobes. Some of the blooms are large, measuring 4 or 5 inches across, as in *Allamanda cathartica* var. *nobilis*. These are a bright, clear yellow and have a pleasant fruity smell. The leaves of this species come in whorls of 3 or 4; they are of a thin texture and hairy, especially on the undersides. It is a strong, tall climber and often seen in hot-houses.

There are several favourite varieties (which are sometimes listed in the trade as separate species), viz. *grandiflora*, with lemon-yellow or primrose-yellow flowers. It is of rather bushy habit and a good plant for a large pot. It needs grafting on the type plant.

Var. *schottii*, a free flowerer; a large yellow bloom with the throat striped with rich brown; most effective as a roof climber.

Var. *hendersonii* has orange-yellow flowers tinged with brown, with 5 light spots in the throat; the lobes, of wax-like texture, are beautifully formed.

Var. *williamsii*, one of the loveliest, has yellow trumpets about 3 inches long and 2 inches in diameter across the top; within, the colour is a deeper yellow, stained with brown. This variety has wiry stems, slender, dull green, and red on the side exposed to the sun. It is a dwarf climber and admirable for growing in a pot where it can be kept to bush shape on slender wooden supports.

A good potting compost for the *Allamandas* consists of 3 parts turfy loam, one part sifted leafmould, one part coarse sand or wood charcoal. They like ample moisture and a humid atmosphere; it is necessary therefore to spray them frequently with tepid water.

Most of the species were introduced into Britain from South America about the middle of the nineteenth century.

Antigonon leptopus is very rarely seen in this country, but is one of the most beautiful of climbers; it has small bright rosy-red flowers, 6 to 15 carried in a raceme, which, as already mentioned (page 17) ends in a branching tendril. Perhaps from the shape of the tiny ovalish flowers, the plant gets one of its popular names, viz. Bride's Tears. In this country, it needs a heated greenhouse, full sun and a good rich soil, but it seldom blooms freely.

In the Deep South it is prized as an outdoor climber for covering verandas and fences; some of the finest specimens (both the type and the white var. *albus*) are to be seen in Florida, where it is one of the most popular of ornamental climbers and often called the Coral Vine. The species was introduced from Mexico in 1886.

Neither this climber nor the *Allamandas* are so well known, I imagine, as the Bougainvilleas, which also come from tropical and sub-tropical America.

Bougainvillea glabra and its varieties are the most useful, for they can be grown in a cool greenhouse and are amenable to pot-culture – they make slender dwarf climbers about 12 inches high.

Their most striking character is the large, showy bracts, purplish in colour, which always astonish one by their richness and brilliant colouring when seen for the first time.

In a greenhouse this species is often planted in a large pot of rich, loamy soil and given a trellis against a sunny wall to climb up. (Like the *Allamandas*, Bougainvilleas need plenty of sun.) It will attain a height of 10 feet or more and grow as much in width. The leaves are bright green and smooth; the bracts, pointed, and a bright rose colour. In a small pot it can be trained on twigs and kept to a height of 12 inches. A glorious pot-plant.

Var. *sanderiana* is a very free-flowering form and gives a magnificent show of deep rose bracts even when it is grown in quite a small pot. Planted in a greenhouse border, it will grow quickly to a height of 20 feet.

Var. *cypheri* is singled out as the showiest of the varieties: the bracts are a gorgeous deep purplish-rose and come freely on all the stems.

These *Bougainvilleas* may be seen growing at the base of boundary walls of gardens near Nice, facing the Mediterranean. They are quite hardy there as they are in other warm climates. In the U.S.A., in the Deep South, they are trained on the verandas of houses, trailing over the wooden balustrades and climbing up the porches. In Britain, unfortunately, they would not survive the cold, damp winter weather.

B. spectabilis, with rose-coloured bracts (varying to deep purple and a curious greenish colour) and thick, green, hairy leaves, climbs by means of its strong hooked spines, as does the brilliant crimson-coloured *B. lindleyana*. The finest specimens of these two species I have seen in heated greenhouses.

Occasional doses of weak liquid manure should be given to the plants during the growing season. All weak shoots and dead wood must be cut out when the flowering season is past.

The genus *Bougainvillea* was named in honour of Louis Antoine de Bougainville, a French navigator (1729–1811).

Cobaea: yet another family of climbers from tropical America. (The genus was named for the Jesuit Spanish priest, Father B. Cobo, 1572–1659, who worked as a missionary and naturalist in Mexico and Peru for many years.)

Out in the garden they are best treated as annuals (they are easily raised from seed); indoors, where they are protected from frosts, they are perennial. A loose, fairly rich loam suits them best: in a pot or a tub it should be richer and the plants will flower more freely. The best known is *C. scandens* (scandent, climbing), which in the warm gardens of the South will climb up to a height of 20 feet or more by means of its leaf-tendrils (see page 17 and Fig. 2, page 16). (The leaflets come in 2 or 3 pairs, and instead of a terminal leaflet there is a branching leaf-tendril.)

The flowers are bell-shaped, about $1\frac{1}{2}$ inches across at the mouth, with protruding stamens, and greenish-violet in colour. They bloom from July to October.

There are two varieties, viz. var. *flore albo*, with white flowers; and var. *variegata*, which has leaves variegated with creamy-white. I have not seen these two varieties in gardens, but the type plant is fairly common. It was introduced into this country towards the end of the eighteenth century.

The wide, prominent calyx at the base of the corolla (bell-shaped) has been likened to a saucer; the corolla to a cup. Hence the popular name, the Cup and Saucer Plant.

A slender bamboo cane is the best support for it in a pot. Outside it will climb up slender twigs or trellis-work and is often used to trail over an archway.

Greenhouse specimens should be pruned back after they have flowered; young growths will shoot up in the spring. New plants raised from seed sown in heat in spring will be required for outdoors.

Cucurbita is the family of Gourds, cultivated mostly for their singular fruits which ripen and colour in the autumn and can be collected then and used for indoor decoration during the winter.

They climb by means of their tendrils (2- or 3-branched), which shoot out of the long, running stems.

C. pepo (one-celled: many-seeded) and its varieties are the kinds usually grown in our gardens; they are eminently suitable for training across the roofing beams of wooden pergolas, which are perhaps temporary, rather flimsy structures. (They always seem to me a little out of place on a big stone pergola.)

Var. *aurantia* has fruits the shape, size and colour of an orange which are most effective when they can hang down from horizontal wooden beams.

Var. *ovifera* has pear-shaped fruits; and var. *verrucosa*, whose fruits are edible, has egg-shaped warted fruits.

They are annual plants; the seed should be sown in heat in early spring.

C. maxima is another annual Gourd with ornamental fruits in a variety of colours. They are round in shape – sometimes very large as in the form *C. maxima* var. *sylvestica*, which has fruits as large as a man's head. (It is found wild in regions of the Himalaya.)

The important thing, of course, is to get the fruits to ripen and colour; therefore seed should always be sown as early as possible in heat so that the plants are ready to put out in May – or earlier, in the south.

The best soil is a light, sandy loam.

Habitat: tropical regions of Asia, Africa and America.

Cucurbita is an old Latin name for the Gourd; in medical language the word means a cup or cupping-glass shaped like a Gourd.

Several Ivies are suitable for growing in small pots. The tender species *Hedera canariensis* needs protection. The form var. *variegata*, which has its leaves edged with yellowish-white, and the type plant are two favourite foliage climbers for growing indoors. The potting-compost should be fairly rich and must be kept moist. There are several ways of training the stems: a single stem may be tied to a slender stick about 12 inches high and grown like this for several years; or 3 or 4 stems may be allowed to grow and trail over the side of the pot, which should then be placed in a container (best on a wall) where they can show off the leaves to advantage.

The common Ivy, *Hedera helix* and many of its varieties have become popular plants for pots.

H. helix conglomerata is a slow-growing, dwarf form, the leaves crowded and small. Var. *marginata* represents several attractive forms whose leaves are margined with white or yellow – *marginata rubra* is particularly attractive in the autumn, when the edging turns rosy-red.

Var. *minima* is the smallest of the varieties, its leaves crowded, $\frac{1}{2}$ to 1 inch across.

Var. *pedata* (the Bird's Foot Ivy) has 5-lobed leaves, the middle lobe long, narrow and finger-like.

All these Ivies can be grown in quite small pots and left undisturbed for many years.

Ipomoea is a genus of twiners, annual and perennial, the most popular in this country being the annual *I. purpurea* (often described by botanists as *Pharbitis purpurea*). It has open, bell- or funnel-shaped flowers, blooming from July to September, and broadly heart-shaped, downy leaves, 3 to 5 inches across. There are many garden forms, varying in colour. They are appropriately named: viz. *alba*, white; *azurea*, sky-blue; *tricolour*, whose flowers are striped red, white and blue.

Var. *Dickensonii* has blue flowers, and *flore-pleno*, double ones.

I. purpurea, commonly known as the Morning-Glory, is best raised from seed (it can be bought in packets from any seedsman), and sown in pots. Use Thumb pots (one-inch pots) and sow a single seed in each; the plants can then be knocked out when the soil is dry, without disturbing the roots. Pot-bound plants will bloom more quickly. Soak the seed in warm water for a few hours before sowing; they should be planted early, under glass; or put the pots on a window-sill in a sunny room.

These annual twiners like a rich, leafy, moist loam and full sun. They can be grown up strings, wires or a wire trellis. In a warm, sheltered garden they will go up to a height of 10 feet.

As a pot-plant the Morning Glory is much in demand and can be kept to a height of about 2 feet by pinching out the top shoots. A slender bamboo cane is the best thing for it to twine round.

I. purpurea, a native of tropical America, was introduced into Britain in 1629 and first described in the *Botanical Magazine* as *Convolvulus purpurea.*

Ipomoea, according to Linnaeus, is from *ips,* bindweed; and *homoios,* like or similar; the plant resembling the creeping convolvulus. L. H. Bailey states: "Ipomoe-a: Greek combination, *worm-bindweed,* of no particular significance."

Lapageria rosea. I have seen flowers on the plant at Kew in December. It grows in a shady part of the Temperate House, its slender, hard shoots twining round its supports; and at that time of the year its evergreen, leathery leaves (1 to 4 inches long) are its greatest attraction.

This plant is not suitable for a pot, but I have seen it grown in a tub and stood on a veranda, close to the house wall on which wire trellis was fixed for the plant to climb up. It thrived and flowered well in that position for many years.

The ideal place for it is a cool, shady greenhouse; and an arch-like structure of some sort, where the stiff shoots can be trained across the top, would be most suitable; for the flowers will hang down away from the foliage; they are less conspicuous on a wall.

In some parts of Cornwall and Devon, especially in warm, maritime districts, *Lapageria rosea* is a success outside on a shady wall. It goes up to a height of 10 feet or more and will bloom through the summer and the autumn. It is not often damaged by frost.

The flowers, a rich crimson, spotted rose, are bell-shaped, 3 inches long and 2 inches wide at the mouth, and of a waxenlike texture. There is a charming variety called *albiflora,* which has unspotted, white flowers; it makes a fine companion for the type plant.

Lapagerias like a leafy, loamy soil (3 parts sifted leaf-mould or peat, one part turfy loam, and one part coarse sand) and plenty of moisture during the flowering season.

They are natives of Chile and were introduced to Kew in 1874. The common name is the Chilean Bellflower.

The genus was named in honour of the Empress Josephine, *née* Tascher de la Pagerie.

Passiflora coerulea (blue). This is the Passion-flower, which so many gardeners aspire to grow. It can be grown on a warm wall in some parts of the country but it is sometimes killed by frost. Better to grow it in a cold greenhouse, if we treasure the plant – and it is uncommonly beautiful with its open Clematis-like flowers, white with a conspicuous purplish centre.

The name Passion-flower (*passio*, passion; *floris*, flower) originated with the early Spanish missionaries in South America (the habitat of the plant), who imagined they saw represented to them in the flower the instruments of Christ's Passion.

The flat, open flower, slightly fragrant, is from 3 to 4 inches wide and is composed of 5 sepals and 5 petals, white touched with pink; the purplish ring of thread-like growths in the centre is known as the corona. The leaves, often evergreen, are deeply divided into 5 lobes and measure from 4 to 7 inches across.

This beautiful tendril-climber is a slender plant (rather delicate-looking, when raised from seed under glass) but extremely vigorous, going up to a height of 20 feet on a trellis against a wall.

Ordinary well-drained sandy loam suits it best; and it must have plenty of water throughout the growing season. It is one of the finest climbers for a pot and will give a copious display of flowers in a cold greenhouse from early June to August. Plant it in a 12-inch pot of good loam and start it climbing on tall, slender Beech twigs; it will soon reach the roof and grow along wires or strong cords, supporting itself by its wiry coils of tendrils. The tendrils of Passion-flowers are long and much more delicately constructed than a thick leaf-tendril of, say, the Clematis. They are shaped like spiral springs and grasp a suitable, slender object (such as a wire or a string) by their forked ends. The coil formed by the tendrils keeps the plant as it ascends firmly attached to its supports and at sufficient distance to prevent any friction between it and the stem. Passion-flowers like full sun.

There are few climbers that are so easily raised from seed; it should be sown under glass in March, and the seedlings pricked out when they are about 1 inch high.

The species, a native of Southern Brazil, was introduced into Britain about 1699.

The variety 'Constance Elliott' was introduced by the Nursery Lucombe, Pince & Co., of Exeter, in 1884, and has large, fragrant, ivory-white flowers.

Passion Fruits are seen in some of our shops. The species which bear the most popular kinds are *P. edulis* and *P. quadrangularis*; the former, dull purple when ripe, is about the size of a hen's egg; the latter, brownish-yellow, are ovalish and often 8 inches long. The pulp of *P. edulis* is often used in South America to prepare a refreshing drink: it is beaten up in a tumblerful of iced water to which a pinch of bicarbonate of soda is added.

Plumbago capensis, native to South Africa, introduced into Britain in 1886, is grown for its glorious azure-blue flowers, and needs the protection of a greenhouse if it is to bloom freely. It is a semi-climbing plant which, in a pot, can be trained up tall twigs or bamboo canes and gives a lovely display of blue in summer. The flowers come in spikes; the individual bloom has a very slender tube ($1\frac{1}{4}$ inches long) and lobes similar to those of the Phlox. Usually in a greenhouse where it will be safe from frost, it is allowed to climb up trellis or pillars. In the warm parts of the world it climbs trees and is left undisturbed.

The species likes a fibrous, peaty loam and when it has finished blooming, it should be pruned back hard and kept fairly dry through the winter.

In warm, sheltered southern gardens, the plant could be sunk in its pot by a wall and trained on trellis; but it must be housed again during the winter.

Plumbago is from an old Latin name meaning lead or lead-like: its application is uncertain: it may refer to the lead-coloured flowers of some species.

Quamoclit. A group of twiners not common in this country. Yet species like the scarlet *Q. coccinea* and *Q. pennata* are so striking in the vivid colouring of their flowers that they should certainly be grown when seed can be obtained. *Q. coccinea* (scarlet) can be kept to a height of 3 feet in a pot (twining the plant round a cane); or outside in a hot, sunny spot it may go up to 20 feet or more. It is best treated as an annual and raised each year from seed. The flowers, fragrant, are small, funnel-shaped, broad at the mouth, and an intense shade of scarlet. They come in great abundance and are conspicuous against the deep green pointed leaves. The popular name of the plant is Star Ipomoea. (The *Quamoclit* are sometimes included with the *Ipomoea*.)

Q. pennata (leaves pinnate). The flowers, small, fiery-red, are narrow and funnel-shaped, about 1 inch long; and the leaves deeply pinnatifid (herring-bone fashion) are delightful in their shape.

It may be grown in a pot and kept quite dwarf or transplanted from the greenhouse and set out in a row against a fence facing due south. It needs full sun. Any ordinary garden soil suits the *Quamoclit*. The origin of the word is *kuamos*, kidney-bean (Greek).

Rhodochiton atrosanguineum (very dark, blood red). A tender annual climber which supports itself by its twisting flower- and leaf-stalks; and goes up to a height of about 10 feet. The dark blood-red flowers, about 2 inches long, are roughly tubular-shaped, with 5 prominent lobes. The flowers are solitary; and the calyx, broadly bell-shaped, is reddish and adds to the beauty of the flower. The leaves are heart-shaped and about 3 inches long. A lovely climber for a pot; it will bloom the first season from seed.

Thunbergia alata, commonly known as Black-eyed Susan, is usually treated as an annual and in the greenhouse is often planted in pots or hanging-baskets. A hairy twiner, with yellow-cream, trumpet-shaped flowers with a dark centre. In our warmest maritime districts it may be grown in the garden, but should not be planted out till fairly late – seedlings should be thoroughly hardened-off first.

The species, introduced from South Africa in 1822, is readily raised from seed sown in a greenhouse during March or April. A rich medium made up of equal parts of loam, peat and decayed manure is most suitable for this tender climber.

There are several varieties: var. *alba* has white flowers; var. *aurantiaca*, deep yellow; both with dark centres. Var. *lutea* is completely yellow; and var. *sulphurea* a charming shade of sulphur-yellow.

Tradescantia: the name is well known to most people who grow pot-plants. The species, nearly always called by its popular name Wandering Jew, is *T. fluminensis* (the epithet means "growing in running water"), which trails over the sides of pots and is a charming foliage-plant for hanging-baskets. In darkened rooms or where the light is dim, the leaves are green; but in full sunlight they become reddish-purple underneath. There are forms with lighter, and with white and mauve-striped, leaves; the variegation is more pronounced in plants grown in full sunlight. The plant must have plenty of water if it is to grow regularly. It is suitable only for the greenhouse or for indoor decoration.

Propagation is by cuttings, which root very readily. Most people who grow the plant have pulled off pieces of the stems and set them in a pot, where they have rooted in a short time.

Tradescantias are natives of North and tropical America. The genus was named for John Tradescant (died 1638), who was gardener to Charles I.

The *Tropaeolum* genus is represented in most gardens by *T. majus* which is the common Nasturtium – one of the gaudiest twiners we can grow. It is often allowed to scramble up trellises and is very showy trained on strings or wires against a wall, especially when a different variety is chosen for each string: a scarlet, then a yellow, then a dark purple, and so on. There are many ways of growing these annual climbers. If several are planted out on a sunny bank, they will soon cover it with their brilliantly-coloured flowers; and the sandier the soil, the better the show. In rich soil or on moist, sunless sites, growth of stems and leaves will be at the expense of flowers. A bank which gets sun on it all day is ideal.

In a pot the semi-climber 'Golden Gleam' makes a fine decorative plant if it is trained on bamboo canes or beech twigs. Nasturtiums are sometimes grown in tubs to give a show of colour in a small town garden. Half a dozen plants of the same variety are set round the edge and trained up bamboo canes, converging and tied together at the top to form a sort of wigwam-shaped structure.

Seeds may be sown where the plants are to bloom, or they may be brought on in pots and the seedlings put out in May.

T. majus, a native of Peru, was introduced into Britain in 1686.

T. peregrinum is the Canary Creeper, a tall twiner (also from Peru), with small, sulphur- or lemon-yellow flowers. The leaves are 5-lobed, the lobes deeply cut. It is a tall climbing plant which grows quickly and, like the Nasturtium, can be used in many ways. In hanging-baskets it is especially decorative; the trailing stems if too long can be pinched at the ends. Other plants of contrasting form and colour (the sky-blue, bedding Lobelia, for example) are often associated with it and set in the middle of the basket.

The Canary Creeper, much less showy than the Nasturtium, is easily raised from seeds.

Another *Tropaeolum*, a perennial species, is *T. speciosum*, known as the Flame Flower or the Flame Nasturtium. Its flowers, similar in shape to those of the common Nasturtium but much smaller, are a vivid scarlet. Unfortunately, it proves an intractable plant in many gardens. It needs a cool, shady position and lime-free, peaty soil which never dries out. It seems to flourish luxuriantly in most Scottish gardens. A particularly striking effect is to be had when it is allowed to ramble over a black-green Yew – it should be planted on the north side of the Yew and provided with some sort of ground cover such as a dwarf shrub or one or two boulders to shade its roots or rhizomes. These should be set 9 inches deep and left undisturbed. *T. speciosum* is not normally suitable for a pot but it does very well in a shady coldhouse, where, on a wire-trellis, it will give a rich display of colour in late summer. A native of Chile, it was introduced into Britain in 1846.

There are one or two Vines which are sometimes grown in pots for indoor decoration. More often than not they are planted out in prepared beds in a greenhouse and given trellis to climb up. Some writers include them in the genus *Vitis*; but they are usually now described under *Cissus*.

The Kangaroo Vine, *Cissus (Vitis) antarctica*, native to Australia, needs a warm greenhouse during the winter and revels in cool, dark places. It can be grown in a large pot with slender sticks for the tendrils to grasp or in a bed of loamy soil against a shady wall covered with trellis. It is described in the *Botanical Magazine* (t., 2488), the popular name appearing there as the

Kanguru Vine. The note on the coloured plate of an upper, flowering shoot reads, "The reason our figure does not represent any tendril, is because in the branch from which our drawing was taken, the peduncles (flower-stalks) all bore flowers, in which case the tendrils are of course wanting, these always having their origin in abortive peduncles.

"Native of New South Wales, and known in our gardens by the name of the Kanguru Vine. Introduced into Kew Gardens in 1790, by Sir Joseph Banks. It is a hardy greenhouse plant, only requiring to be kept from frost."

More attractive than this species is *Cissus adenopodus*, with 3-foliolate leaves, 3 to 6 inches long, green above and red beneath. It grows quickly, climbing up slender supports by means of its tendrils. It likes full sun and is a native of tropical Africa (Uganda). A fine foliage Vine for a large pot. Greenhouse protection is necessary during the winter.

The most decorative is *Cissus discolor*, a native of Java (introduced into cultivation in 1854) and invariably grown in a greenhouse in Britain. It is commonly called the Trailing Begonia because of the colouring of the leaves. They are a bright, velvety green above, marked with silvery-white, and reddish-purple beneath; pointed and ovalish in shape. It is a tendril-climber which needs a warm greenhouse and one of the easiest plants to grow, provided it is given a rich, fairly moist loam (equal parts of turfy loam, sifted leafmould and coarse sand).

Tradescantia is probably the favourite pot-plant these days and seems to have ousted the *Aspidistra* which is seldom seen now on its stand or small window-table. The *Tradescantia* is easily grown in a small pot and may be put in a special container and used as a trailing wall-plant. It takes up very little space, which is something to be considered nowadays, and there is not a trailer or climber that can be so readily increased by cuttings. They root in a few weeks.

CHAPTER THREE

Rarer Climbers and Some Wall Shrubs

SEVERAL rare climbers were described in Chapter one but they belonged to families of plants well known to the average gardener, viz. *Clematis*, *Jasminum*, *Rosa*, etc. The following are mostly from families not often met with in our gardens – few people know the tendril-climber *Eccremocarpus scaber*, for example, or the twining *Actinidia*. They may be seen at our Botanic Gardens and can be bought from most shrub specialists. They are all beautiful plants. The shrubs are included because they need the protection of a wall if they are to flower well; and some perhaps wouldn't survive our cold winters if they were planted in the open garden. Many are completely hardy, but bloom from November onward and need a wall to protect their flowers from frosts and cold north-east winds.

The first on our list is a shrub which in these islands must be grown in the south and is mostly planted against a wall. *Acacia dealbata*: its common name is Mimosa, the fluffy, tiny, ball-shaped yellow flowers, sprays of which are seen piled up in the florists' in January. It is often left in its boxes. It is sold so quickly that it is hardly necessary to put it in water. But at home the sprays must be kept in water, if they are to last in flower.

Most of it comes from districts near Cannes and other places in the South of France, where the plants are perfectly hardy and grow out in the open away from walls.

In these islands the best specimens I have seen grew against houses facing due south and overlooking the Channel. The shrubs were tall, reaching almost to the eaves; and others were overtopping the boundary walls against which they grew.

This *Acacia* has been tried in gardens near London but has never succeeded, so far as I know. A shrub was planted against a south wall in the garden at Brampton House, Marlow, Bucks., some years ago. The owner kept it covered with a blanket during severe spells of cold weather, but it never survived.

The best place for Mimosa outside our warm maritime gardens, is the cool greenhouse: it will thrive and flower there as it does in the Temperate House at Kew.

It is evergreen, the fern-like foliage covered with a silvery-white down is uncommonly beautiful and a good foil to the panicles of tiny fluffy yellow flowers. The plant often begins blooming in late summer, but its normal time is autumn and early winter.

The species is a native of Australia and Tasmania, where it goes up to a height of 100 feet and makes a thick trunk 10 feet or so in girth. It is a favourite tree for street-planting and commonly known as the Silver Wattle.

Acacia is from the Greek *akakia*, meaning a thorn. Theophrastus (born B. 372 B.C.) in *Historia Plantarum* mentions *Akakia* (*Acacia*) *arabica*i the Gum Arabic Tree, which is armed with sharp spines 3 inches long. The epithet *dealbata* means covered with opaque white powder. Both foliage and stems are glaucous.

Actinidia is a genus of deciduous twiners which are not often seen in English gardens. Most nurseries list 3 or 4 species in their catalogues and recommend them for pergolas and for covering old trees, etc. The best *Actinidia* I have seen was the quite hardy *A. kolomikta* growing in a coldhouse. It was planted there, not because it is tender, but because the owner prized its pinkish-white variegated foliage, which outside was often spoiled by wet and grime. It is a slender climber from Manchuria, China and Japan and needs bamboo canes or tall twigs to support its stems.

The largest leaves (roughly heart-shaped) are 6 inches long and about 4 inches wide, purplish when young and becoming variegated with white or pink later in the season.

This twiner may be seen at the R.H.S. gardens at Wisley, where it goes up to a height of 20 feet on a wall and has small, white, fragrant flowers in June.

David Fairchild, the plant collector, described a specimen of *A. kolomikta* in his book *The World was my Garden*. It belonged to a friend of his, who grew it in a greenhouse and after many months discovered that the plant was much relished by his cat, which ate the leaves and stems. In the garden plants had to be protected by wire-netting to prevent them from being clawed to pieces. (*Kolimikta* is the native Amur name for the plant.)

Other species offered by our nurseries are *A. arguta* (sharply notched or toothed). A vigorous, twining plant which grows well on trees and has dark, lustrous green leaves (ovalish-oblong: 3 to 5 inches long, sharply toothed) and small greenish-white fragrant flowers in June and July. The greenish-yellow berries are about 1 inch long and edible. They are rather flavourless, I think; but they are apparently enjoyed by the Japanese. The species is native to Japan, China and the Amur region.

A. chinensis (from China). Regarded as the most beautiful of all the species for the garden; it has the largest flowers, 1½ inches across, white at first, then yellowish; the leaves are large, heart-shaped, 9 inches long and almost as wide.

The fruits, which taste rather like gooseberries, are about the size and the shape of walnuts.

The plants are usually unisexual, and when fruit is wanted, it is necessary to grow plants of different sexes together; they are obtainable from most nurseries.

It is less vigorous than *A. arguta* and ideal for training on pergolas and over arches of trellis-work where it will twine its stems tightly round the slender pieces of wood or wire.

A. chinensis, a native of China and Japan, was introduced into England in 1900 by Wilson, who collected it in the province of Hupeh, China.

A. polygama (having polygamous flowers: flowers of either sex or of both sexes on the same plant). It is commonly known as the Silver Vine and, like *A. kolomikta*, is grown for its beautiful leaves. I have seen them marked with yellow or with silvery-white. The plant goes up to a height of 20 feet. I think it looks best on a pergola. It is a native of North-east Asia, Central China and is abundant in mountainous regions of Japan.

Actinidias like a fairly rich loamy soil which doesn't dry out, and thrive in partial shade. They may be propagated by seed, cuttings or layers.

Akebia (the Japanese name of the plants). A genus of two twiners. They are occasionally seen in our gardens and may be obtained from most shrub specialists. *A. lobata* is deciduous; and *A. quinata* evergreen in mild winters and in our warmest gardens. They are both strong growing plants and will twine their stems round any slender supports. They may be trained over shrubs or up trees or on trellis against a shady wall (they like a partially shaded spot). They have little floral beauty; but their foliage is attractive and certainly their curious, sausage-shaped fruits are – when they ripen; but unfortunately they seldom appear on plants growing in this country. The finest Akebias will be seen in the South of France and in Northern Italy. Both species, however, are completely hardy. They like a good rich loamy soil.

A. lobata (lobed) has leaves composed of 3 leaflets, shallowly lobed, measuring 1 inch to 4 inches long. The flowers are purplish and come in pendulous racemes about 3 inches long. Male and female flowers appear together, the former small and numerous; the latter, about 2 in number, large, and a deeper shade of purple. The plant blooms early in April and consequently the flowers are often damaged by frost. Seldom, then, are the fruits seen in this country.

In warm countries where they do ripen, the largest are 5 inches long and about half as wide, sausage-shaped; pale purple first, then they split open in late summer and reveal rows of black seeds embedded in white pulp – they are curious and quite decorative. The species, a native of China and Japan, was introduced to Kew in 1897.

A. quinata (with 5 divisions). Merchant's catalogue states, "Distinct from *A. lobata* in having leaves composed of 5 leaflets; flowers pale purple in short racemes, fragrant. Both species do well on shady walls."

The flowers are richly fragrant and on good flowering specimens can be smelled some distance away. Unfortunately the plant doesn't bloom freely in this country. It is a strong twining plant, going up to a height of 30 or 40 feet in mild districts and is often planted on an old fruit tree.

The species is a native of China, Japan and Korea. It was first introduced by Robert Fortune in 1845, who found it growing on the Island of Chusan, South-east China.

Both plants can be propagated by layering the long stems in spring; or cuttings of fairly ripened shoots may be taken in late summer. These should be given a gentle bottom heat.

Araujia (a native South American name). A genus of about 12 twining plants natives of South America. In our country they are not hardy enough to give a good display of flowers in the open, the species *A. sericofera* (syn. *Physianthus albens*) being about the only one grown – and that won't survive for long in most of our gardens even when it is trained up a wall. I have not seen it listed in any catalogues for years; but Hillier used to have it and described it as "The White Bladder Flower of Brazil. Vigorous, evergreen climber, suitable only for the mildest localities. Flowers in July, white, with a tinge of red, fragrant."

It thrives in a cool greenhouse, provided one keeps an eye open for the mealy-bug, which often attacks specimens growing under glass.

The species is a vigorous twiner with pale green leaves, wedge-shaped at the base, the largest 4 inches long and about half as wide; they are covered with pale grey down beneath. The sappy shoots, which grow long and quickly in a season, are similarly covered and when cut exude a milky juice.

The flowers are small, white, slightly fragrant, and come in clusters, rather resembling those of the Stephanotis; they bloom in late summer. The fruits, which ripen in autumn, are large grooved pods containing seeds with tufts of silky hairs 1 inch long attached to them.

Cruel Plant appears as a common name of the species in some books. The name is used for many plants whose flowers entrap insects. A moth which visits this *Araujia* at night is caught by the pollen and unable to extricate itself till the sun shines on the flowers.

The literal meaning of *sericofera* is "bearing Eastern stuff": silky substance, for example, found on seed capsules, etc. The species was introduced into cultivation in 1830.

Aristolochia. A large genus widely distributed over the temperate and warmer regions of the world. Not more than half a dozen species are known in this country, however – at least in the open. Some have enormous flowers and may be seen in hothouses in Botanical collections. Those of *A. goldieana*, for instance, measure about 2 feet long and 1 foot wide, greenish without and deep yellow with chocolate veining within. The smell of some of these exotic kinds is intolerable – in fact they stink.

Current catalogues list about 3 hardy species. The best known is the Dutchman's Pipe, *A. macrophylla* (large leaves) or, as it often appears in books, *A. sipho* (tubular). Bean, *Shrubs and Trees Hardy in the British Isles*, describes it under this name. (The plant was mentioned, page 15, when the different movements of twining stems were discussed.)

It gets its familiar name from the shape of the flowers; which are about 1½ inches long and bent like a siphon. The tubular part is yellowish-green; the flat expanding lobes are brown and pale purple. The leaves, large and pale green, measure up to 10 inches in length.

It is a rampant, deciduous twining-plant, the large heart-shaped leaves making it attractive when the flowers are over. These come in June. A fine twiner for tall shrubs or for a pergola – it goes up to a height of 30 feet and is completely hardy. The species is a native of eastern North America.

Other species listed in catalogues are *A. altissima*, not quite hardy: not often seen; *A. moupinensis* (from Moupin, China), described as the most beautiful of the *Aristolochia*; the tube is pale green, the lobes yellow dotted with purple-red. *A. tomentosa* has downy leaves, the tube of the flowers is greenish-yellow and the throat purplish-brown.

These twiners (popularly known as the Birthworts) like a loamy, peaty soil. They are easily increased by division. Cuttings of *A. macrophylla* do not root readily and the plant is often raised from seed.

Asteranthera ovata is a rarity and does not appear to be listed in any catalogues. No doubt it is difficult to accommodate in the average garden, for it is an inhabitant of dense forests (Chile), revelling in cool, moist leafy soil and shady places. In its habitat it attains a height of 10 feet or more, attaching itself to trunks of trees and old stumps by its aerial roots. It is an evergreen, with roundish-oval leaves and rich red flowers, which mostly come in pairs. They are tubular at the base, 1 inch long, 5-lobed and 1½ inches wide across the top.

As it is a self-climber, one would expect to see it more often in the warmer parts of our country. It should be grown on a north wall or against a tree in a woodland.

The plant flowers in June and is propagated by seed or by cuttings.

Asteranthera is derived from *aster*, star; *anthos*, flower: the star is the lobed part of the corolla.

Berberidopsis corallina (the Coral Plant). Like *Asteranthera ovata*, it is an inhabitant of the forests of Chile; but it is more tender than that plant and needs the protection of a wall in most districts. Many gardeners buy it for their greenhouses and grow it on a shady wall, giving it a trellis to climb up. It is a twiner and needs assistance, however; without a trellis, on which the long, leading shoots must be trained, it will have to be supported by wires nailed into the plaster.

It is sometimes trained on shady walls in gardens around London; but this is a little too far north for it to bloom freely. Outside Cornwall and other warm regions, there are few places where it will give a good show, unless it is adequately protected throughout the winter months.

It needs a peaty, rich soil, at least to start with and will not thrive where lime is present. Once it is established its roots will find sufficient nutriment in an ordinary sandy loam.

An old plant will go up to a height of 20 feet or more and measure as much across on a north or an east wall.

It is evergreen; its heart-shaped leaves, dark green above and pale beneath, are from 2 to 4 inches long and attractive all through the year. The flowers, at their best in late summer, come in terminal racemes, each flower roundish, ½ inch wide, and of a dark crimson colour. The flower-stalks are red; and the mass of red hanging blossoms against the dark green foliage is a wonderful sight indeed. (The flower-buds as they appear in the illustration in the *Botanical Magazine*, t., 5343, look like small blood-red berries.)

The Coral Plant was discovered in the forests of Valdivia (Chile) and introduced into England by Robert Pearce about 1860.

It can be bought at most shrub specialists. Marchant's catalogue describes it: "An ideal climber for sheltered shady walls and it will even ramble among Rhododendrons in the south and west. Its beautiful drooping racemes of coral-red or dark crimson Berberis-like flowers are a grand sight from early August to October."

Young plants should be raised from cuttings or by layering the long stems in sandy peat.

Bignonia capreolata or *Doxantha capreolata* is a climber which supports itself by its branched-tendrils which adhere to rough surfaces such as that provided by an old brick wall. The curved tips of the tendrils, which turn away from the light, seek crevices and fissures, creep into them and bury themselves in them. Then, by a thickening process of the tips, which swell out like a ball, they fill the crevice and become firmly attached. The tendrils then coil up like miniature, elongated wire springs as they do in the Passion-flower and other tendril-climbers. It is interesting to watch these plants during rough, windy weather, the elasticity or 'give' in the coiled tendril enabling them to move outward from their support as the wind disturbs them. I have seen several good specimens of this *Bignonia* growing in our southern counties. Some on old flint walls; others on Oak-trees. (This climber avoids smooth surfaces.) The flowers are roughly funnel-shaped, about 2 inches long and 1 inch wide at the top, orange-red, and come in clusters in the leaf-axils.

The leaves are composed of 2 leaflets from 2 to 5 inches long, the branched-tendril coming from the top of the leaf-stalk where, in many plants, a terminal leaf grows. (See Fig. 12).

Common names of the plant are the Trumpet Flower, Quarter Vine and Cross Vine; the last refers to the cross-like structure of the stem when it is cut through.

Billardiera longiflora. (The name commemorates Labillardière, a French botanist, who did much valuable research work in Australia and published a work on its flora in 1804.) An evergreen twiner which will climb up trellis and give a fine show of dark blue oblong fruits in October. Its small yellow flowers, tube-like, are pendulous on slender stalks but not striking. The plant is grown specially for its beautiful fruits which come abundantly on specimens grown in warm countries. The leaves, lance-shaped, measure from 1 inch to $1\frac{1}{2}$ inches in length.

It will need the protection of a wall in most parts of this

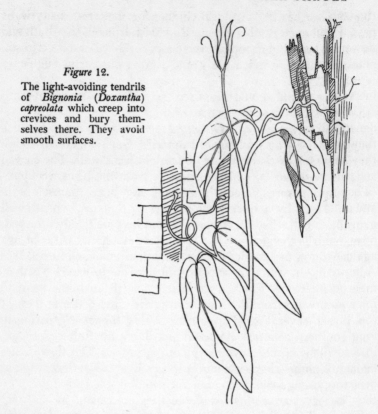

Figure 12.

The light-avoiding tendrils of *Bignonia* (*Doxantha*) *capreolata* which creep into crevices and bury themselves there. They avoid smooth surfaces.

country. In Devon, Cornwall and Southern Ireland it is perfectly hardy and may be trained over bushes in the open garden. I have seen it growing up walls about 5 feet high – a very charming dwarf blue-berrying twiner. A native of Tasmania and introduced in 1810. Most nurseries supply it and the white-berried form *fructo-albo*.

Calystegia japonica belongs to the family *Convolvulaceae* and is a strong climber which will twine its long shoots round slender-stemmed bushes or clamber over old tree-stumps in the wild garden, which is the ideal place for it. The convolvulus-like flowers are a bright pink and bloom during the summer and the autumn. On trellis-work it will go up to a height of 20 feet or so, but as it is rather difficult to control, it is inclined to look rather untidy. The leaves, hastate (halberd-shaped) are attractive and provide a flowing mass of green when the flowers are past. I particularly like the double form var. *flore-pleno*, whose flowers (2 inches long and completely sterile) have long, wavy petals, flesh-pink at first then bright rose.

Any ordinary soil suits these Calystegias. They are easily increased by root-division.

Camellia are evergreen shrubs well known to most gardeners, many of whom would like to grow them but do not, they state, because they have no greenhouse. In cold districts they certainly need housing, but around London they thrive and bloom well when planted against a north or a west wall. (They are, or most of them are, completely hardy in Cornwall and other parts enjoying a mild climate.) There are two ways of growing them in more northern districts: they may be planted near a sheltering wall, say, 3 or 4 feet in front of it; or close against it in the same way as *Viburnum fragrans* is often grown. Admittedly old-established plants have a top-heavy look, the main stem growing up flat against the brickwork and naked for about 4 feet and all the foliage and flowers coming at the top. But at least one is assured of a good show. And if the wall is long enough and a dozen plants can be set next to one another in a row, a beautiful and unusual effect of massed flowers will be had. A wall with a north or a west aspect is best, for the soil beneath will be cool and moist, which is what Camellias enjoy; they will be protected too from blustering winds.

The variants of *C. japonica* are the best known, the most suitable for outdoors being the single and semi-double red ones, which appear to suffer less from frosts than the very double kinds. 'Apollo', bright red, semi-double, with yellow stamens, is an old favourite – excellent on a wall. There are dozens of others equally beautiful; nurseries will supply lists.

Some of the varieties will be in bloom by early spring; and those grown close against the wall will give the finest display. Throughout the summer the glossy evergreen leaves are attractive and, where there is a border in front, provide a pleasing background for summer flowers.

C. sasanqua and its variants have smaller leaves and flowers than the Japonicas and bloom earlier; they are often at their best in November; the small pinkish flowers of some smelling deliciously of tea.

Camellias need lime-free peaty soils and mulching with rotted leaves in April. They are natives mostly of China and Japan.

Campsis. Two species are known in this country and offered for sale by nurseries; they are often listed under *Tecoma. Campsis chinensis*, native to East Asia, climbs up to 20 or 30 feet on a warm wall, which it must have if it is to bloom well in our gardens – it gives a better display in the south, especially in Italy and the South of France. The trumpet-shaped flowers, about 3 inches long and as wide, come in terminal, pendulous panicles of 6 or 12 and are deep orange and red in colour. Very striking against the green leaves. The plant should be tried on a white-washed wall. *C. chinensis* is not self-supporting as is the other species and needs tying to a trellis or nailing on a wall.

C. radicans (rooting) has aerial roots, though they are not so tenacious as those of the Ivy; large plants often need some support. (I suggest a wire trellis for it, which it will soon cover.) It is more vigorous than the other species and hardier.

The flowers are trumpet-shaped, rich scarlet and orange, not quite so large as those of *C. chinensis*, but very showy. The leaves are composed of from 7 to 11 leaflets, smooth and dark green above and downy beneath.

Both species (and the different varieties) like a good loamy soil.

When the wall space is sufficiently covered, they may be pruned annually by cutting the growths back to 2 or 3 buds of the old wood in winter.

C. radicans is a native of the south-eastern United States and was known in our gardens as long ago as 1640. Propagation is by cuttings of fairly firm wood, which should be taken in July. They will root quickly under glass.

Ceanothus is a large genus of deciduous and evergreen shrubs and small trees confined to North America; they are from California, Colorado and New Mexico where they live and flower in hot sunshine.

In our country they are nearly always grown against warm, sunny walls; and we have come to look upon them as a group of choice, blue-flowered wall shrubs. The blues are good (most of them): pale shades and dark, often free from purplish tints. There are white- and pink-flowered kinds, which are perhaps not so well liked.

The summer-blooming kinds are hardier than the spring bloomers and can be grown in the open garden. The hybrid 'Gloire de Versailles', with fragrant, powder-blue flowers in late summer and autumn; and 'Burkwoodii', rich blue, are well known.

The evergreen *C. papillosus* blooms in May and has small panicles of flowers an exquisite pale blue colour. It is best on a wall in most of our gardens and will go up to a height of 10 or 12 feet and spread out into a glorious covering of blue. The leaves are long and narrow and have conspicuous excrescences known as papillae on the upper surface. A native of California.

Another early-blooming evergreen species from California is *C. thyrsiflorus*; it is, however, much hardier than the above species and suitable for growing on a wall in our colder gardens. It is listed in Hillier's catalogue where it is described as "The hardiest evergreen Ceanothus, forming large bushes up to 20 feet high in the open at Kew. An excellent wall shrub for northern counties. Flower-panicles often 3 inches long; of a powder-blue shade."

The ovalish leaves are about 1½ inches long and glossy green; the flowers come in clusters from the leaf-axils and are at their best in May.

I think the variety *griseus* is equally attractive, though the flowers are a lilac-blue – an exquisite colour, however; and the leaves are larger and broader and grey beneath. But it is not quite so hardy as the type plant.

C. veitchianus, introduced from California in 1853, is thought to be a hybrid between *C. thyrsiflorus* and *C. rigidus*. The flowers come in dense heads about 2 inches long and are a glorious bright blue; its glossy green leaves are a perfect foil and a cheerful sight covering a wall in winter.

Ceanothus like a well-drained light loamy soil and are increased by cuttings of half-ripened shoots taken in July. They need a gentle bottom heat and should be well rooted by the following spring.

Celastrus. Two or three species are grown in our gardens: *C. orbiculatus* and *C. scandens* are about the most popular. They are twiners, planted for the beauty of their fruits which ripen in the autumn. Their flowers are small and insignificant – greenish or yellowish-white.

C. orbiculatus, from North-east Asia, is a vigorous climber which twists its long stems round the branches of trees and goes up to a height of 30 or 40 feet. If it is planted in a deep, rich, loamy soil, it will establish itself quickly and need little attention apart from cutting off long unwanted growths.

The leaves, 2 to 5 inches long, vary in shape; they are usually round (orbicular) and turn golden-yellow in the autumn. The fruits, shaped like a pea, are green at first; when they ripen, they turn a bright orange-yellow and later split open and reveal their brilliant scarlet seeds.

A mature specimen laden with these fruits is one of the most colourful climbers we can have in our gardens during the winter months. The seeds are apparently not liked by birds and often remain on the branches till late January. A berrying twiner that deserves a place in every garden.

The species was introduced into this country by Professor Sargent of the Arnold Arboretum who sent seed to Kew in 1870.

The plant is usually allowed to climb over trees and shrubs, but some gardeners have grown it on pergolas; and it is most effective clambering up string netting fixed on a south wall (as I have seen it). But I think something more permanent is necessary for such a strong, vigorous twiner.

C. scandens (climbing) was the first of the family to arrive in this country, having been introduced by Peter Collinson in 1763. It is a native of North America, where it is prized at Christmastime for its berries which are as decorative as those of the other species. The plant fruits more freely in the wild than it does under cultivation, though it makes a good splash of colour in Cornwall and Devon during the autumn and the winter. As practically all plants are unisexual, both male and female specimens should be grown together to ensure the pollination of the flowers and the production of fruit.

The species is a feature of the woods on Goat Island above Niagara Falls, where during the autumn shrubs and trees are hung with masses of the vivid orange and scarlet fruits.

Both species are obtainable from shrub nurseries. Propagation is by seed or by layering the stems.

Chaenomeles lagenaria usually appears in catalogues under *Cydonia japonica* and is called affectionately the *Japonica* by many gardeners. In nine cases out of ten it is planted on a wall and will bloom there as early as December if the weather is mild. It is probably the most popular of all wall shrubs with amateur gardeners and gives very little trouble. It gets untidy, however, if the long, interlacing stems are left unpruned; these should be cut back in late summer, removing the new growths and leaving the old wood, which carries the flowering spurs, untouched. The plant is not a climber as some people imagine it to be; it has no tendrils, nor do its shoots twist or twine; grown in the open garden, as it often is, it makes a big, round shrub 10 feet or so high and twice as much through, but does not bloom so early and often not so well. Planting it against a wall or a fence is an artificial way of growing it, but the usual way in most of our gardens.

The lovely apple-blossom-like flowers are well known and, as already stated, come on the leafless shoots sometimes as early as Christmas. They measure about 1½ inches across and are carried in clusters on the old wood. In this district (South Bucks.), the favourite variety seems to be the one with pinkish-white flowers called var. *alba*. The type plant has scarlet or red flowers; and there are many named varieties sent out by the nurseries. Some of the best known are: *Abricot*: semi-double, orange-red; *atropurpurea*: dark crimson; *cardinalis*: deep salmon red; *nivalis*: pure white flowers; *rubra grandiflora*: large, crimson flowers. My own favourite is *Knaphill Scarlet*, which has rich orange-scarlet flowers.

The dark glossy green leaves are usually well-advanced before the show of flowers is over.

These flowering Quince like a well-drained, loamy soil and are perfectly hardy. (The species which bears the fruit used in making jams and tarts etc., is *Cydonia oblonga*.)

The shrubs should never be disturbed once they are planted, for they seldom recover after a move. Propagation is by suckers or by layering some of the long, untidy branches.

Chimonanthus praecox (early) often appears in catalogues as *C. fragrans*. The generic name is from *Cheimon*, winter; *anthos*, flower. The shrub is commonly known as the Winter Sweet: an appropriate name, for its flowers are deliciously fragrant and although not showy are a delight during the dead season from November to March.

It is an old favourite and mostly grown against a wall where it ascends to a height of 10 or 12 feet. The plant is deciduous, the flowers appearing on the naked shoots, which should be brought up close to a window. They have a purplish centre and yellowish outer segments and measure about 1 inch across. The leaves, a dark lustrous green, are oblong-shaped, 3 to 6 inches long and about half as wide.

The Winter Sweet prospers in ordinary garden soil and on a wall should be pruned (when the stems get too long) in March, so that new flowering growths are made early in the year.

In the open garden, where it does not grow so tall, it scarcely needs any pruning.

Two *Clematis* species which were not included in the list given in Chapter one are *C. calycina* and *C. indivisa*, both ever-green. The former is a winter bloomer; the latter rather tender; they therefore require the protection of a wall in most gardens in this country.

C. calycina (having a conspicuous calyx) is commonly called the Fern-leaved Clematis on account of its finely-cut foliage; it is an attractive bronzy colour during the winter and dark green during the summer months.

The flowers in a good form measure about 2 inches across; they have 4 sepals, yellowish and downy outside and stained inside with reddish-purple spots. The conspicuous cup-shaped organ beneath the sepals is called the involucre and distin-guishes the species (as it does in the related *C. cirrhosa*) from all the other hardy species. The flowers are nodding, solitary, on stalks about 1 inch long and when they come freely are very charming through the dull winter months. A north wall is best for this Clematis. On a south wall, where it is often planted, the frosted flowers are nearly always damaged by the early morning sun before they have a chance to thaw out. The plant grows to 15 feet and when covered with its yellowish nodding flowers is a cheering sight on a grey January day. Often, especially after a hot summer, the flowers begin to open in September and continue to come through the autumn and the early winter.

A good deep mulching of sifted leaf-mould is beneficial to this species and should be applied during April.

Pruning of the mass of tangled stems is rather a task and is best deferred till the plant has got too large for the place allotted to it. It should then be cut back to strong healthy stems.

Layering is the easiest method of propagating the plant.
Most nurseries stock it: it is usually listed under its synonym
C. balearica.

It is a native of the Balearic Isles. Introduced to Kew Gardens
in 1783 from Paris where it had been in cultivation for some
years.

C. indivisa (undivided: the leaflets are often entire). In its
habitat, New Zealand, this lovely evergreen Climber clambers
over tall shrubs and trees, covering them with masses of pure
white flowers, which have yellow stamens and rose-coloured
anthers. It is a pity it cannot be grown outside in all our gardens,
for it is one of the freest-flowering of the Clematis species.
Probably Cornwall and other warm south-western regions are
the only parts of the country where it will succeed. Bean mentions South Surrey: a plant grows and flowers well in a garden
there. Another flourishes luxuriantly in woodland at Exbury,
Hampshire. But around London the species needs housing. And
it never fails then to give a glorious show of blossom; a single
plant, well established, may easily carry thousands of open
flowers at one time. Professor Sargent of the Arnold Arboretum, Massachusetts, once described a greenhouse specimen
which had 7,000 open flowers.

The flowers are about 3 inches wide, composed of 6 to 8
narrowish sepals and come in panicles 4 to 12 inches long. They
are larger on the male plant than on the female. The leaves have
3 leaflets (entire or sometimes lobed) measuring from 1 to 3
inches long.

It is a vigorous climber in the wild, very common and widely
distributed in New Zealand, where it was discovered during
Captain Cook's first voyage. The plant was introduced into
England in 1840.

The variety *lobata* has deeply lobed leaves and, like the type,
blooms in May. A beautiful plant may be seen in a cold greenhouse at Kew Botanic Gardens.

Both forms are obtainable from shrub specialists.

Clematoclethra. A small genus of climbing shrubs rarely seen
in our gardens. And very seldom offered by nurseries. *C. integrifolia* appeared in an old catalogue of Hillier's. "Rare, scandent
shrub from North-west China. Flowers, white, *clethra*-like.
Probably not hardy in cold localities." It is thought to be only

a form of *Clematoclethra actinidiodes* and has small white, fragrant flowers, solitary or in clusters. It goes up to a height of 20 feet or so and is usually planted against a tall shrub. The plant is described in the Journal of the R.H.S. for August, 1936. "Native of Kansu and Szechwan, China. A climbing shrub, hardy in sheltered positions in this country, with axillary fascicles of small white or pinkish flowers from which the long style is exserted, variable ciliate-dentate leaves, and reddish-black berries."

C. scandens is perhaps better known: a climbing shrub up to 20 feet tall, with clusters of small white flowers which come from the leaf-axils. The leaves vary in size: the smallest 2 inches long by 1 inch wide; the largest are twice as big; they are bristly on the margins and on the veins. The fruits are small round, red berries. It needs the protection of a wall in most districts. Both plants like an open, loamy soil.

Clianthus puniceus is the Parrot's Bill of New Zealand, a glorious climbing shrub unfortunately not hardy in many districts in the British Isles. It needs a warm climate such as it gets in California, where some glorious specimens are grown in Golden Gate Park, San Francisco. The hanging clusters of brilliant red flowers look magnificent against the dark green fern-like foliage. The individual flower is constructed similarly to the pea-flowers, though it is very different in appearance: it has an erect petal about 2 inches long and a 'keel' slightly longer; from this curved or canoe-shaped 'keel' the plant gets its popular names Parrot's Bill and Lobster Claw.

The leaves are from 3 to 6 inches long and composed of from a dozen to about 25 small leaflets, dark green above, paler and slightly downy beneath. It is a wonderful climber for warm districts. Those who have room in a cool greenhouse should certainly grow it.

I have seen it grown in large pots and trained up bamboos round the edge.

Outside it needs an open, loamy, well-drained soil.

Propagation is by seed sown under glass or by cuttings rooted in sand with bottom heat. Most shrub specialists stock the plant. In Hillier's 1955-56 catalogue it was described, "The 'Lobster Claw'. Handsome but tender New Zealand scandent shrub, with semi-evergreen, pinnate leaves. The large, scarlet flowers, of peculiar shape, are carried in clusters during summer.'' The plant was then priced at half a guinea.

Clianthus is from the Greek *Kleois*, glory; *anthos*, flower; and *puniceus* means crimson.

Cocculus trilobus is a twiner noted chiefly for its ovalish or heart-shaped leaves which remain on the plant till late in the year – they are sometimes 3- or 5-lobed. The plant has little floral beauty, but the round berries, $\frac{1}{4}$ inch in diameter, which come in clusters of from 6 to 12 are attractive when they ripen and become blackish-blue. They are most abundant after a hot summer. Any ordinary soil suits it. It is easily propagated by seed or by root-division. It will go up to a height of 12 feet or more of trellis.

The species is native to Japan, Korea and China and can be supplied by most shrub specialists.

Cotoneaster horizontalis is often referred to as a climbing shrub. Its branches are arranged horizontally, 'fish-bone' fashion up the stems, which push upward to a good height when

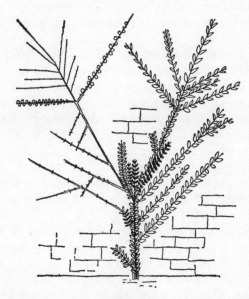

Figure 13.

Wall used as a support for the Lattice-forming stems of *Cotoneaster horizontalis*.

the shrub is grown against a wall, without actually making any contact with it. The plant may be 10 feet tall or more in such a position. But it is not a true climber. In the open it spreads itself out and will cover rocks many feet in width. It is seen to best advantage against a wall and is a reliable winter-berrying plant.

The leaves are crowded on the stems and fall very late, the terminal ones retaining their glossy green colour, the others turning orange and red. By December, when the plant has shed its foliage, the stems are bright with small, globose, red berries, which make it such a valuable ornamental wall shrub. The beauty of the berries is enhanced by the yellow flowers of the Winter Jasmine (*Jasminum nudiflorum*); the two grown side by side on a west or a north wall are a feature of many a town garden. And it would be difficult to find an association that is so bright and colourful during the dullest weeks of the year; moreover both plants grow in any ordinary soil.

This Cotoneaster has little floral beauty; the flowers are pinkish-white and tiny and may pass unnoticed.

It is increased by cuttings taken in late summer.

The species is a native of China and can be got from any nursery.

The two species of *Decumaria* are climbers which support themselves by aerial roots. They are not hardy and therefore grown only in our warmest regions: they are used in Cornwall and Devon to cover walls and look very pretty with their panicles of small white or yellowish-white flowers (fragrant) in June or July.

D. barbara, native of the south-eastern United States, introduced in 1785, goes up to a height of 30 feet in the wild where it flowers freely. Its fruits are urn-shaped, striped with white and a feature of the plant when they are borne in large quantities.

The ovalish, pointed leaves, from 3 to 5 inches long, are a refreshing shade of green and make the plant a worth-while climber to have. But I have not seen it or the other species in any gardens outside Devon and Cornwall.

D. sinensis is evergreen (the other species usually deciduous) and a valuable plant in being one of the few evergreen self-clinging climbers that are grown in this country. Less vigorous than the other, it seldom goes up above a height of 10 feet.

It does best on a partially-shaded wall and makes a mass of interlacing stems and smooth, shining green leaves. The flowers, small, yellowish-white, in clusters 3 inches long are not conspicuous. The plant gives a much better show in the wild, when it is covered with flowers which are apparently very sweetly scented.

Henry, the botanist, who discovered it in the Ichang Gorge, Hupeh, Central China, described it as a creeping plant, "hanging down from the walls of cliffs with beautiful clusters of fragrant, white flowers". It is not so fascinating a plant under cultivation. Gardeners who grow it describe it as being about 5 feet high and 7 feet wide.

Wilson introduced it in 1908. Both species do well in good, loamy soil. Their nearest allies are the climbing Hydrangeas and the Schizophragmas.

Eccremocarpus scaber is a half-hardy woody climber, which supports itself by the much-branched tendrils which come from the ends of the main leaf-stalks. It produces plenty of seed and in most districts is treated as an annual. Seed is sown under glass in February; the seedlings are potted up and planted out in May, the plants flowering about 6 weeks later. In warm, sheltered gardens facing the sea, this climber will live for many years, growing 5 or 6 feet high and clambering over bushes, covering them with tubular, orange-red flowers. These are about 1 inch long, 10 or 12 being carried in racemes 6 inches in length. The leaves are pinnate or doubly-pinnate, the leaflets measuring from $\frac{1}{2}$ to 1 inch long.

It likes a fairly rich soil, especially when cultivated in a cool greenhouse, where it is perennial.

Its common name is the Chilean Glory Flower; a native of Chile, it was introduced in 1824. The plant is offered for sale by most shrub nurseries. Marchant's catalogue describes it as a fast-growing climber, a biennial in cold districts. "But in warm gardens and around the sea coast, it survives for a number of years. From June to October, it produces numerous 1-inch tubular orange-peel-coloured flowers. A specimen on a sheltered trellis near here (Wimborne, Dorset) is a splendid sight every summer."

Ercilla spicata (spike-like) is also a native of Chile and an evergreen provided with aerial roots. On vertical surfaces, however, old plants, with their tangle of heavy stems, often need supporting by wires. The ovalish, fleshy, glossy green leaves (about 1 inch long) are its greatest attraction and a welcome sight through the dull winter months.

The flowers, dull white and small, come in dense clusters about 1½ inches long during March and April. When freely carried, they stand out conspicuously from the thick foliage but they are not particularly beautiful.

Hillier's listed the plant in one of their catalogues under the specific name of *Ercilla volubilis* (twining).

Euonymus radicans is common enough in our gardens, where it is sometimes used as a ground cover in sunny or shady places and on banks where little else will grow. It is also planted on walls, up which it climbs by means of its aerial roots and it will attain a height of 20 feet or more, covering the brickwork with dark green small leaves about 1½ inches long and half as wide. When it reaches the top of the wall and can no longer climb, it changes its character, as does the Ivy, and produces larger leaves and bears fruit.

It is mostly clipped over in late summer to keep it a pleasant, neat mass of foliage. It is completely hardy and more successful than Ivy in the colder regions of the U.S.A.

There are several variegated forms which are perhaps more popular than the green-leaved plant. In var. *Silver Gem*, the silvery-white leaves are edged with pink; var. *coloratus* has leaves which are a deep purplish-red throughout the winter months.

They may be bought at any shrub nursery.

The best way to propagate these plants is by root-division; the slips will grow very quickly in a shady place.

Exogonium purga (*Ipomoea purga*) is known as the Jalap Plant and has rich rose convolvulus-like flowers which come in September. They come later in some districts and are consequently caught by the first frosts. It is best on a wall. In more sheltered gardens it is sometimes grown at the base of a shrub and sends its stems, often 15 feet long, up through the branches and drapes the plant with flowers. I like to see it best this way.

Jalap is the purgative made from the tubers, which are usually round in shape, mature ones being the size of an orange.

The *O.E.D.* quotes (1876), "Jalap is now grown in the open

air in botanical gardens in the south of England and on the continent." (1866), "Although the best Jalap is obtained from *Exogonium purga*, yet many species of *Ipomoea* supply it, though of an inferior quality." We don't grow the plant nowadays for its Jalap but for the autumnal display of lovely flowers. It needs a good, rich loamy soil.

Feijoa sellowiana is a plant very few gardeners have heard of. It is an evergreen shrub which flourishes in the south, where it is chiefly valued for its red-and-white flowers, which are rather like those of a Fuchsia, the long, protruding crimson stamens giving a rich show of colour when the plant is at its best. It is a native of Southern Brazil and Uruguay and on the tender side, the finest specimens in our country being seen in Cornwall and other warm maritime counties. Nevertheless, it can be grown farther north, if it is planted against a warm wall, though it does not bloom so freely around London as it does within reach of the warm sea air. It does well on a south wall at Kew Botanic Gardens.

The evergreen leaves are ovalish, the largest 3 inches long and almost as wide, dark, shining green above and whitish and felted beneath – an attractive feature all through the year.

The flowers come in July, the petals and sepals reddish-white in colour, and the stamens a rich dark crimson. Each flower is about $1\frac{1}{2}$ inches wide and is carried on a felted stalk.

The shrub needs a light, loamy soil and full sun if it is to prosper. Most shrub specialists have the plant. Marchant's catalogue states: "Foliage deep green, silvery beneath. It bears attractive 2-inch flowers with many protruding crimson stamens, during late summer and autumn. It is usually planted against a south or west wall, but noble specimens growing in chalk soil can be seen in the open."

The genus was named for Don Feijo, a botanist of San Sebastian; and the specific epithet is in honour of the German botanist Sellow, who discovered the species in 1819.

Ficus stipulata is as rare as the *Feijoa* and I have not seen it listed in any English catalogue. It is a climbing Fig (*Ficus*), evergreen, which clings to walls and trees by its aerial roots. A valuable climber, therefore, but grown mostly with us in a cool greenhouse. The plant is perhaps hardier than many people imagine, for it grows and flourishes in the open in Sussex and in Devonshire. It will climb up high walls and retain its small heart-shaped leaves (about 1 inch long) till it tops its support and ceases to climb, when it changes its character completely. Like the Ivy and other stem-rooting climbers, it then attains its adult and fruiting stage, the leaves becoming leathery and bigger (about 3 inches long); and the fruit, which it bears, being of the usual fig-shape.

It is as a climber, however, in its juvenile form, that it is valued and grown in our greenhouses. On shady walls 12 feet or so high, it makes a dense flat mass of dull green leaves. The fruits are decorative when they ripen, being then a deep orange colour tinged with purple.

A native of China and Japan, it was introduced into Britain in 1771.

Forsythia suspensa is a common, hardy shrub that is seen in many gardens: sometimes in the open but more often on a wall; and since the plant blooms early, a north or a west wall is best. Its long, pendulous, leafless branches are often covered with hanging clusters of bright yellow flowers in February or earlier in the south. On a wall, if the plant is to attain a good height, the stems should be supported by wires or tied to trellis. It will grow as tall as 20 feet or more and make a wide-spreading wall plant unrivalled for its display of brilliant yellow. There are often as many as 6 flowers in a cluster, the individual ones measuring about 1 inch across the 4 lobes. The plant may after some years get untidy and need pruning; this should be done immediately the flowers begin to fade.

Branches on some forms of *F. suspensa* trail on the ground and root there. They should be cut off in September and planted out to provide new shrubs, if these are wanted.

All Forsythias need a deep, rich loam and should be liberally fed and mulched every second year.

They are obtainable from any shrub nursery. Hillier lists *F. suspensa* var. *Fortunei*, "A vigorous grower with arching branches. One of the best 'climbers' for a north wall."

Var. *sieboldii* is offered by most nurseries. It was introduced from Japan in 1833 and is of more bushy habit than the type plant; its pendulous branches sweep the ground.

F. suspensa is a native of China but was first introduced into Europe from Japanese gardens.

The genus was named in honour of William Forsyth, superintendent of the Royal Gardens at Kensington (1737–1804).

Garrya elliptica is fairly well known but more commonly seen in our southern gardens where it does better than in the north. It is best given a sheltered place in gardens near London and makes a fine ornamental wall shrub for the winter months.

Apart from the evergreen foliage, its chief attraction is the slender hanging catkins which in warm climates are as much as 12 inches long. They are graceful and lovely from November till March and come in clusters from the leaf-axils. The flowers, of which the catkins are composed, are a silky greyish-green (cup-shaped bracts enclosing the base of the stamens) and much larger on the male plant than on the female – it is usually the former that is planted.

The leaves are ovalish, the largest 3 inches long, the margins waved, dark, shining green above and paler beneath.

A charming ornamental shrub for a wall. Specimens of either sex can be bought. The female plant is much less striking, the catkins seldom exceeding 4 inches in length.

The Garrya likes a light loam, perfectly drained and full sun. It must not be disturbed when once established; it often does not survive transplanting.

The popular name is the Tassel Bush. A native of California and Oregon, it was introduced by the collector Douglas in 1828, who named the genus in honour of Mr. Garry of the Hudson's Bay Company, a promoter of much of the collector's research work in North America.

Hedera is the family of the Ivies,[1] the species *H. helix* being the common sort, indigenous to Britain and most parts of Europe. It can be seen in our woods, where it creeps over the ground among the undergrowth and climbs trees, attaching itself to the bark by strong aerial roots. In gardens it is similarly used and from the ground it climbs up a wall or a fence and is sometimes planted on a house. Opinions about its use on house walls differ: it is said to keep old cottages warm and dry; but some people condemn it because its mass of evergreen leaves hold the wet after heavy rain, which causes damp to infiltrate through to the inside plaster. Walls of old flint cottages are

---

[1] *H. helix* is not one of the 'rarer' climbers; but there are several species which are seldom seen in our gardens. All kinds are listed here together.

usually thick and consequently always dry; but single brick walls may be affected by the overgrowth. Cavity walls are not affected.

Ivy is aesthetically pleasing only when it is kept well under control: when it is permitted to spread round the base of a wall, for example, and is nicely pruned into shape. When it covers a house wall completely (as we often see it) from the base to the eaves, it is ugly. And too often it is allowed to become a disfiguring overgrowth on ancient buildings, covering up much of the architectural design and in time perhaps ruining some of the delicate and intricately-carved work.

It is best, I think, in the garden and will grow most luxuriantly in shady, damp places, though practically any soil, site and aspect suit it.

Trees are only damaged and killed by it when it reaches the uppermost branches and covers the bark and the young growths, preventing thereby the breathing functions of the tree. And at this point, when Ivy can no longer climb, it attains its reproductive state. Its stems, which no longer have any aerial roots, branch out and produce larger, unlobed leaves, flowers and berries. If cuttings are taken and rooted (they root readily in sandy soil), bush Ivies or 'Tree-ivies' as they are called may be raised in quantity. They retain their bush-like character permanently.

Gerard refers to the creeping or climbing type in his *Herbal* (1597). "Creeping or barren Ivy is called in English 'Ground Ivy'."

The Common Ivy (*Hedera helix*) has sported into many varieties, some of which are listed in nurserymen's catalogues and are sometimes seen in our gardens.

What we may regard as the typical form has three- or five-lobed leaves, about 3 inches long, a dark green colour, with paler veins; the leaves give off a strong, unpleasant smell when crushed. The flowers of the 'tree' type come in the autumn and are carried in clusters; they are of a yellowish-green colour. The fruits, which are more decorative, are black, globose berries, measuring about $\frac{1}{4}$ inch across.

Ivy stands any amount of clipping and pruning; but it is hardly necessary to touch it at all in most places in the country. In towns, where the foliage is soon soiled by soot and smoke, an occasional clipping-over is beneficial. The new leaves are fresh and glossy and pleasant to see. Clip the plants in March.

Several varieties of the Common Ivy were mentioned in the preceding chapter on pot-climbers; they are hardy enough to be grown outside and deserve to be more widely planted. Var. *minima*, the smallest-leaved, is the best choice for limited spaces and may be used in the rockery. Var. *angularis aurea* is one of the golden-leaved varieties and is listed by Hillier as the best of its kind. Var. *deltoidea* has leaves more triangular in shape than most of the varieties and they assume a pretty bronze shade in October. Var. *ovata* is outstanding by reason of its ovate, almost entire, leaves; they are of a rich green colour and very slightly lobed even in the climbing state. In var. *purpurea* the leaves are a purplish colour through the winter months. Many of the coloured forms are apt to revert to the common green type after some years; but as they are easily propagated by cuttings or by layering, they can be renewed every so often.

The other species of Ivy are less often seen in our gardens and some are quite rare. *Hedera canariensis* (the Canary Island Ivy, native of the Canary Islands and North Africa) is tender and it and its variety *variegata* are often grown in pots in a cool greenhouse (see the previous chapter). The type plant has large leathery leaves, three- or five-lobed, which measure from 2 to 8 inches wide. Its fruits are black as in *H. helix*.

The variety *variegata* is better liked on account of its attractive colouring: the leaves are a dark green in the centre, the colour merging into a creamy-grey which is margined with white. A favourite pot-ivy.

Var. *azorica* is a vigorous form from the Azores and has vivid green, five- or seven-lobed leaves which, in their young state, are covered with a thick tawny felt. In the variety *azorica variegata* the leaves have a broad margin of white. These Ivies all do well out of doors in our southern maritime gardens.

H. chrysocarpa: the yellow-berried Ivy from Italy and Greece. The leaves are triangular or ovalish and shallowly-lobed or entire; those of the fruiting plant are often diamond-shaped and always entire. It makes a pretty 'tree-ivy' when in full fruit.

H. cinerea is the Himalayan Ivy; its leaves have a decided greyish tinge to them – the plant is sometimes called the Grey-leaved Ivy. They are long and taper-pointed, spear-shaped; and the berries are either yellow or red. Not a particularly robust Ivy in all gardens and best on a wall. It is found wild in different parts of the Himalayas.

H. colchica is a native of the regions south of the Caucasus (collectors have found it in Georgia) and of Northern Persia – its common name is the Persian Ivy. It is the largest-leaved species; the leaves are leathery, ovalish or heart-shaped, 3 to 7 inches wide and often 10 inches long, slightly lobed or entire. A very fine foliage plant for a wall, the dark, lustrous green leaves showing up well on red brickwork. In the variety *dentata* – sometimes called the Giant Ivy – the leaves are coarsely-toothed. Both plants like a fairly rich, moist soil and will grow rapidly when they are once established. Two of the most handsome of all the Ivies that can be grown in our gardens.

H. hibernica is said to grow wild in Ireland and the west of Scotland. It is listed in catalogues as the Irish Ivy and differs from the common *H. helix* in having larger and paler green leaves. The plant is mostly used as a ground cover in moist woodlands where it grows rapidly. On walls it looks rather coarse compared with the other Ivies and gardeners prefer to let it have a free run in suitable shady places. It looks particularly fine on old oak-trees.

H. rhombea, known as the Japanese Ivy (it comes from Japan and Korea) is of dwarf habit: a slow-growing, delicate-looking Ivy, but quite hardy and very charming on a wall. The leaves are variable: triangular, ovalish, usually three-lobed; and in the variety called *H. japonica variegata* they have a thin border of white. Both Ivies make delightful pot-plants, they are easily trained up slender bamboo canes.

Hedera is an old Latin name for Ivy; *helix* an old Greek and Latin name for a twining-plant.

Hibiscus: the name evokes the hot sunny lands of the Mediterranean; and it is there that the shrub flourishes most luxuriantly; but good flowering specimens can be seen in many of our southern gardens, and the best of them are usually grown against warm walls. They seldom give a good show of flowers in the open garden in places north of London. There are many species, but the one cultivated here is the deciduous *Hibiscus syriacus* and its many varieties.

The specific epithet is misleading, for the plant is native only to China and India, where it grows into an enormous shrub with erect branches, 20 feet or more high, covered with trumpet-shaped flowers (5-petalled), the largest measuring 4 inches across. They come singly on short stalks, the colour in the different forms being very variable. The leaves are toothed or lobed, ovalish-shaped, the largest measuring about 4 inches in length.

Hibiscus like ordinary garden soil, well-drained and full sun on them all day. They are specially valuable in our gardens, giving us a show of flowers in September, which is rather late. There are single varieties, which top the list with most of us who know the shrubs, semi-double and double kinds. All of them do much better during a hot summer.

Some of the loveliest varieties listed by nurserymen are the following. 'Admiral Dewy', pure white, double. 'Coeleste', single purplish-blue. 'La Reine', rose-coloured, single flowers. 'Monstrosus', large single white flowers with a dark purplish-rose centre. 'Rubis', magnificent single ruby-red flowers. 'Totus albus', single pure white artificial-looking flowers: the best white variety I know.

During a warm spell of autumn weather the flowers come successively from September to the end of November.

Cuttings of all these Hibiscus root readily under glass. Many gardeners, however, prefer to layer the shrubs. They can be got from most nurseries; and some are supplied in standard form. The common name of the Hibiscus is the Tree Hollyhock.

Holboellia. The genus was named for F. L. Holboell, who was at one time superintendent of the Botanic Gardens at Copenhagen. Two species are grown in our gardens; neither is well-known; they are evergreen and therefore among the most valuable of climbers. Both are twining plants and secure themselves permanently to trees and shrubs or trellis by their long stems.

H. coriacea is hardier than the other species, *H. latifolia* (though both seem to do best on walls), and will climb up to a good height when it settles down in places that suit it. The leaves, of a leathery texture, are composed of 3 leaflets, the largest 6 inches long by 3 inches wide; the flowers are greenish-white (male) and purplish (female: these are also larger) and come in separate clusters during April and May; the purplish-coloured fruits (2 inches long and 1 inch wide) have jet black seeds. The species, a native of Hupeh, China, was introduced by Wilson in 1907. At Kew, where this twiner bloomed for the first time in 1921, it was much admired and regarded as a valuable addition to the few evergreen climbing plants we grow in our gardens. It is quite capable of growing on trees, but most gardeners prefer to train it up trellis-work on a wall.

H. latifolia, less hardy than the other, may be distinguished from it by its leaves, which have 5 or more leaflets. They are a dark, glossy green, of a leathery texture, and handsome all through the year.

The flowers are very fragrant, male (greenish-white); and female (purplish and more conspicuous) coming in clusters from the leaf-axils. This species is native to the Himalaya, from where it was introduced more than a hundred years ago. The natives of those parts eat the fruits, which are said to be very palatable. They are sausage-shaped, about 3 inches long and contain numerous seeds. Gardeners in this country usually fertilize the flowers by hand. On the whole the finest specimens of these climbers are to be seen in our cold greenhouses, where, too, the scent of the flowers is much stronger. Hillier's catalogue lists both species as being on the tender side.

Hydrangeas are usually thought of as highly ornamental shrubs for borders. There are, however, two or three climbing species grown in this country; they have whitish or yellowish-white flowers (but not unfortunately 'hydrangea-blue' colour) and are mostly found in large gardens where they can spread themselves out on high walls.

The first is the least known: *H. anomala,* which attaches itself to tree trunks by aerial roots and reaches a height of 40 feet or more in the wild. It is deciduous and often listed in catalogues under the synonym *H. altissima.* Its habitat is the Himalaya and China; in mountainous parts of Western Yunnan it has been found growing as a shrub up to about 10 feet high; other specimens have been seen climbing over bushes and carrying big, attractive flower-heads: the flowers are rather colourless and insignificant on some forms in cultivation. The best have large, white, sterile ray-flowers (about 1 inch across) which come round the margins of the small yellowish-white fertile flowers. The heads measure about 6 inches across; and the flowers are sometimes fragrant.

Specimens of this climbing Hydrangea which I have seen in our gardens have had smaller flower-heads (not particularly striking) and the flowers have been scentless.

This climbing Hydrangea blooms in June and gives a better show in the south than it does, say, near London. It is closely related to *H. petiolaris*, which is more widely planted. *H. anomala* was introduced here in 1839 but has never become popular.

H. integerrima is the most valuable of the three climbing Hydrangeas we grow in this country, since it is evergreen, and its tough-looking leaves give a pleasing show of dark glossy green all through the winter. Its flowers are not very showy but when they come freely, as they do in our southern gardens, the massed greenish-white inflorescences, somewhat columnar-shaped, are pleasing to see against the foliage. The bushy shoots produce the flowers: the climbing ones are sterile. On a low wall, then, it makes a delightful evergreen covering; and in the south, where it prefers a shady spot, it may be used as a climber on tall trees, to which it will cling, like the others, with its strong aerial roots.

In nature it climbs up trees 50 feet tall, topping them with lacy, white flower-heads, and scrambles over rocks, where it flourishes just as luxuriantly. The species, a native of Chile, was first grown in Britain from seed sent home by the botanist Comber in 1907.

It has been grown successfully on a shady wall in cool greenhouses, but is hardy enough for outside culture in many districts.

The species is rarely offered for sale by nurseries. Marchant described it as a little-known self-climber, useful for low walls, rocks, etc. "In the south it loves shade."

H. petiolaris is more striking in flower than either of the other two. It climbs similarly, by aerial roots and is more vigorous, reaching a height of 60 or 80 feet in its habitat (Japan). Under cultivation it is less vigorous, though in the south it will go up to the eaves of a house, perhaps 20 feet or more. In most gardens where I have seen it on a west wall, it has not been above 15 feet tall but more than that in width. Its white, lacy-looking flowers last longer on a north wall and come in profusion on large mature specimens. The inflorescences are flat, from 6 to 10 inches in diameter, and are composed of small, dull white fertile flowers and marginal sterile flowers which stand out conspicuously on long stalks. The leaves are roundish, toothed (as in *H. anomala*), the largest about 4 inches long, dark green above and paler and slightly downy beneath.

This deciduous, climbing Hydrangea is very beautiful on trees, and may be grown in the open garden, where it becomes bush-like and spreading, and in full bloom is a sheer delight in early summer. The species was introduced from Japan in 1878.

Most shrub specialists stock the plant. Hiller described it as "An attractive, self-clinging climber from Japan, quite hardy and suitable for any aspect. The flowers appear in early summer and are densely packed in flat corymbs 6 to 10 inches across, with a few large white sterile flowers along the margins."

Like the others, it needs a rich, moist, leafy loam. Propagation of these three self-clinging Hydrangeas is by layering or by cuttings.

Hypericum leschenaultii was discovered in the mountains of Java about the beginning of the nineteenth century. *Hypericum calycinum* (the Rose of Sharon) is common enough, but I doubt whether many gardeners have heard of the other. It is best treated as a wall shrub in most of our gardens, though it has been known to succumb to frosts even when it is planted close to one in districts north of London. As far inland as this, it is best perhaps grown in a greenhouse where one can always be sure of a good show of its wonderfully rich yellow flowers, and where, by the way, the foliage will be evergreen. Out in the open the plant often sheds its leaves in winter.

The stalkless, dark green leaves are about 2 inches long and 1 inch wide and glaucous beneath. The flowers measure about 3 inches in diameter and come singly or sometimes in clusters of 3 at the ends of the shoots. They bloom usually from July to the end of September. The colour is such a rich, showy yellow that it is worth giving the shrub a trial against a warm, sheltered wall: an evergreen set on each side of it will afford extra protection and keep it from being damaged irreparably by our damp, wet weather. In warm, maritime districts it will be safe and flower freely and for a long period. Many specimens will be found in these parts growing either against walls, where the plants go up to a height of 10 feet or so, or in the open garden where they are dwarfish.

The plant is of lax habit, the usual method of growing it being to train its upper stems flat against the wall (on wires) and to let the lower ones trail freely in front. In a place which suits it, it will make shoots 3 or 4 feet long in a season.

The species is easily increased by cuttings; and it is worth while to take them every year to have some plants for reserve. This rare wall shrub does well in a loose loam and is stocked by Marchant's nursery.

Kadsura japonica, an uncommon evergreen twiner not completely hardy in gardens around London and needing there the protection of a wall. Farther south and south-west it has been grown in the open garden and has done very well, carrying yellowish-white flowers from about June till the autumn. They come singly in the leaf-axils of the season's growth and are composed of about 6 fleshy petals, the corolla being 1½ inches long and ¾ inch wide. The flowers are not particularly decorative but very pleasing seen against the dark green, pointed leaves (2 to 4 inches long), and it is they, I think, which are the plant's chief attraction; for in October they turn rich red and purple. The berries, when they ripen, are round and scarlet and come in globose clusters.

This evergreen twiner will go up to 10 or 12 feet on a wall and is mostly grown in such a place. It is a member of the Magnolia family and closely related to the Schizandras.

A native of Japan, it was introduced to our gardens in 1860.

There is a variety called *variegata*, whose leaves have a broad margin of creamy-white. I have seen both kinds growing at Hillier's nursery in Hampshire. The plants need a deep, loamy soil.

Kerria japonica var. *plena* is as common as the Kadsura is rare. It is probably seen nearly as often growing against the wall of a house as the yellow Winter Jasmine; as the flowers of the Jasmine fade, those of the Kerria begin to open and go on through April and the beginning of May. The shrub is perfectly hardy but always seems to be grown against a sunny wall – I cannot recall a garden where it is grown in an open border. In cold northern gardens it is certainly best in such a position if the flowers are wanted as early as April. They are well known:

fluffy clusters of orange-yellow petals that come all the way up the erect slender branches.

The leaves (deciduous) are ovalish and about 3 inches: long and coarsely toothed.

A good loamy soil is best for the plant, which needs thinning out (remove some of the old stems) every other year.

I have succeeded in propagating it by half-ripened cuttings inserted in sandy loam out of doors. These cuttings should be taken in July. Every nursery stocks the plant. The genus was named in honour of William Kerr, who introduced the plant from Japan in 1840.

Lardizabala biternata is a rare, tender twiner that is offered for sale by several shrub specialists and when it can be had in bloom is a handsome plant which will go up to a good height. Hillier's described it in a catalogue as "A very distinct, vigorous, Chilean, evergreen climber. Flowers unisexual, purple and white, in drooping racemes. Leaves very variable in form, having 3 to 9 leaflets, of a tough, leathery texture, and bright green colour."

The climber, which belongs to the same group as the Akebia, flourishes in the open on walls in Cornwall and Devon and carries a profusion of flowers at the end of the year. Male flowers, purplish-chocolate and white in colour, come in pendulous spikes 4 inches long; the female are carried singly on slender stalks. The leaflets, which are 2 to 4 inches long, show up the flowers well.

Near London this very charming twiner must be housed and it can be trained up a tall trellis to give a show of flowers for winter. The fruits, which I have not seen, are sausage-shaped, 3 inches long, and much relished apparently by the people of Chile, who gather them and sell them in the markets.

In the South of France this twiner may be seen climbing up the front walls of houses, covering them from the ground to the eaves. The species was introduced from Chile in 1844.

Lippia citriodora is the Lemon-scented Verbena, common in our seaside gardens and liked for the pungent, lemon scent of its leaves. It is a favourite shrub in the Channel Islands. The smell is particularly strong when you rub the leaves between your fingers. The plant cannot be grown well in the open garden near London and nearly always succumbs to frost and damp.

But it is often tried against a south wall and has succeeded there in many gardens. Its leaves are 3 to 4 inches long, about 1 inch wide and pale green in colour. The flowers, small and pale purple, come in downy panicles, about August. In warm maritime gardens the plant goes up to a height of 10 feet or more. In its habitat, Chile, it is a small tree. It was introduced into England in 1784.

Lonicera. There are two bush forms of the genus (Honeysuckle) which are favourite wall-shrubs with many gardeners, viz. *L. fragrantissima* and *L. standishii*. Both are completely hardy but, like most winter-blooming shrubs, do best when planted against a wall. The flowers begin to open about the same time as those of *Viburnum fragrans*, which is November, and during a mild winter will continue to bloom till February or later. In the open garden in this country they are often spoiled by frost.

On a wall *L. fragrantissima* becomes quite tall – up to 10 feet – and although not striking when in full bloom, is one of the most richly-scented things we can grow. Its flowers are creamy-white, about $\frac{1}{2}$ inch long, and come in several pairs at the joints of the stems. It is often evergreen, the leaves being oval and from 1 to 2 inches long, of a stiff, leathery texture. It is best facing west or north-west, which aspects shade the flowers from the early morning sun. During a cold autumn the plant often sheds its leaves, but its flowers come just as freely. A native of China, it was introduced by Robert Fortune in 1845.

L. standishii (Standish's Honeysuckle) is often confused with it; but this shrub has larger leaves (evergreen or deciduous, according to the climate) and are more pointed at the apex; and it has smoother shoots and flower-stalks. The leaves measure up to 4 inches in length and are dark green and rough to the touch. On a wall it will after some years reach a height of 12 feet and when in bloom is a choice winter shrub. The flowers are very similar to those of the other plant: creamy-white and small and come usually in two pairs at each joint. The species was introduced by Fortune from China the same year as the other. Neither plant is as showy as any of the Climbing Honeysuckles we grow, but for their rich scent alone they are well worth a place on a house wall – preferably near a window. Both thrive in a good deep loamy soil.

Most *Magnolias* are hardy enough for the average English garden, but two mostly grown against walls are the evergreen *M. delavayi* and *M. grandiflora* and its varieties. The latter species may be seen at Kew growing in the open and against walls. The ones in the open are much dwarfer than those on the house walls, these specimens running up the front to a height of 20 feet or more and spreading out rather untidily; they want pruning back into shape every few years.

M. delavayi, native to Yunnan, China, is the smaller of the two and if grown in the open garden in warm southern districts, will make a spreading, flat-topped tree some 30 feet high. Tall, healthy specimens can be seen in Cornwall, with their large, greyish-green leaves (glaucous and downy beneath), some as much as 14 inches long and 8 inches wide. The flowers, cup-shaped and fragrant, are about 8 inches in diameter; the petals, dull white, about 4 inches long and 2 inches wide. It is a magnificent evergreen, regarded by many gardeners as the most imposing of any we grow in this country.

The plant should be set 4 or 5 feet away from the wall to enable its trunk and main branches to attain good proportions. Cutting out long, straggling branches will help to preserve the symmetry.

M. delavayi (named for the French botanist Delavay) was introduced by Wilson in 1899.

M. grandiflora (large-flowered) arrived in this country much earlier: round about the beginning of the eighteenth century. It has proved one of the most popular evergreen shrubs for growing against a wall. A south or south-west aspect is best for it: the finest specimens I know have been growing against walls facing due south. But the plant does not flower freely in many gardens – young specimens not at all. Some forms, such as var. *ferruginea*, are said to be more free-flowering than others. Wrong pruning can also prevent the plant from blooming; only superfluous young shoots should be removed (they usually hang outward from the main stem; cut them out, but do not cut into the old, ripe wood, for this produces the flowers).

We are only concerned with it as a wall shrub or tree. It will in time reach from the ground to the eaves and spread out wide, perhaps too wide for most houses; and it is best to plant it on high walls (as we do the climbing Hydrangeas). On cottages it is overwhelming; and often small specimens look out of place.

Even if the plant doesn't flower, the foliage is always good to see. The oval or oblong leaves, from 6 to 10 inches long, are thick, leathery, a dark, glossy green above, and covered beneath with a reddish-brown felt. The flowers, like bowls, are creamy-white and 8 or 10 inches across; they are fragrant – a spicy, fruity smell – and come in August and September.

The following varieties are among the best and may be found flourishing in many parts of the country.

Var. *ferruginea* was reproduced by layering. The undersides of its leaves are covered with a thick, russet felt. The shrub is excellent for chalky soils.

Var. *gloriosa* has enormous flowers, 12 inches in diameter.

Var. *lanceolata* (known as the Exmouth Magnolia) is said to be hardier than the others; and it often blooms when comparatively young. It has large, white flowers and leaves narrower than those of the type.

These Magnolias can be bought from most nurseries.

M. grandiflora is a native of the southern United States, where it grows into a mature tree 60 to 80 feet high.

Like *M. delavayi*, it needs a good, deep rich loam. A little free lime in the soil is not harmful.

Mandevilla suaveolens (sweet-scented) is a tender, deciduous, twining shrub which in warm climates goes up to a height of 12 feet or so and makes a very attractive plant against a wall, where, by the way, it has been tried in gardens just south of London but has not survived. It is best in southern regions near the sea, or housed in a cool greenhouse if it is grown inland.

One of its great attractions is the rich fragrance of its flowers, which is specially noticeable indoors. (The plant is not, however, amenable to pot-culture and prefers a prepared bed against a wall.)

The creamy-white, funnel-shaped flowers come in clusters of 6 or 8 from the leaf-axils, measure 2 inches long and about $1\frac{1}{2}$ inches wide and are at their best in late June.

The leaves, a dark, dull green, are heart-shaped, tapering to a long, fine point; the largest are about 4 inches long and 2 inches wide, and contrast well with the white flowers. In the autumn the plant is covered with crimson seed-pods, which often measure 16 inches in length and are not more than $\frac{1}{4}$ inch wide.

Outdoors it needs full sun, and it should be grown in a light, loamy soil containing peat or leaf-mould and trained on trellis or over sticks.

Mandevilla suaveolens, a native of the Argentine, was introduced to Britain in 1837; the genus was named in honour of Mr. H. J. Mandeville, British minister at Buenos Aires at that time.

Hillier describes the plant as an "elegant slender climber from Argentina. Flowers large, pure white, very fragrant. Only suitable for the mildest localities."

Marsdenia erecta has been cultivated in England since the sixteenth century but because of its tenderness has never been widely planted. It is a deciduous twiner which will attain a height of 20 feet on a warm, sheltered wall but succumbs quickly to frosts if it is planted in the open garden. I have seen it only in a cool greenhouse and was struck by the rich smell of the white flowers, which are quite pretty. They are $\frac{1}{2}$ inch wide and come in closely-packed clusters on the stems in June and July. The greyish-green leaves are about 3 inches long.

The species is related to the twiner *Periploca graeca*, but is not so hardy as that plant. *M. erecta* is a native of South-east Europe and Asai Minor. People who grow it have found that the milky juice which comes from the stems, when these are cut, blisters the skin. The juice is also very poisonous.

Menispermum canadense is the 'Moonseed' of Canada, a deciduous twiner with rich, green, heart-shaped leaves; greenish-yellow flowers, quite inconspicuous; and racemes of black fruits about the size of a black currant. Its leaves are the most decorative thing about it; some gardeners utilize them for covering up unsightly objects such as sheds, by planting one or two specimens at the foot of it. On a pole or a trellis this twiner goes up to a height of 12 or 15 feet and is very attractive when covered with clusters of berries. It suckers very freely and consequently should not be grown near shrubs one values. The species is a native of eastern North America, and has been grown in our gardens since the end of the seventeenth century.

Another species sometimes seen is *M. dauricum,* which comes from North-east Asia and China. It is very like the American plant but not so decorative in fruit. Both may be cut back to ground level at the end of the year; they will shoot up again in the spring.

The single seed within the fruit is crescent- or moon-shaped; hence the origin of the generic name (*mene*, moon; *sperma*, seed).

Metaplexis japonica (often listed as *M. stauntonii*) is another rare climber in cultivation and, like the two previous ones described, belongs to that class of climbers which are most useful for camouflaging unsightly objects standing in some out-of-the-way corner in the garden. These plants haven't much floral beauty, so there isn't much to be missed. This twiner has dull rosy-white flowers, very small, which come in racemes about 4 inches in length. They bloom in late summer and are followed by spindle-shaped fruits, 4 inches long, the seeds having at one end a long tuft of silky hairs. The leaves are a dull green, heart-shaped, the largest being about 4 inches long. One could call it a utility climber and train it over something one doesn't want to look conspicuous. The plant goes up to a height of 10 feet or so and like other soft-shooted climbers dies down during the winter months.

A native of China, Japan and Korea, it was introduced in 1862. Ordinary garden soil suits it.

Mitraria coccinea (scarlet) is described by botanists as a tender, evergreen climbing shrub best grown in a greenhouse. Marchant's catalogue states, "A prostrate shrub or a climber according to position, bearing from June onwards orange-scarlet flowers, like suspended pentstemons. It is not so tender as many people suppose, and well worth trying in semi-shade or on a north or west wall." I have seen it prospering out of doors only in the south of England and there not a very floriferous plant; the few flowers that were carried being of a rich glowing scarlet colour. Housed it does much better and gives a magnificent display of colour in May and June. The flowers are tubular, about $1\frac{1}{2}$ inches long and $\frac{1}{4}$ inch wide, the yellow stamens protruding beyond the corolla. The leaves, a dark, shining green, ovalish and leathery, are small ($\frac{3}{4}$ inch in length) on cultivated plants: much larger on plants in the wild.

This ornamental evergreen climber likes a moist, peaty loam and a shady position if it is to flourish. Near London (at Kew, for instance) it must be grown under glass.

It makes a charming creeper in rock-gardens in Southern Ireland and other places enjoying a similar climate.

The species, native to the Island of Chiloe and other parts of Chile, was introduced into England by William Lobb in the year 1846.

Muehlenbeckia complexa (encircling) is rather more than a 'utility' climber, yet it is frequently planted to cover something up and not much valued by gardeners who grow it. Bean says, "It makes a dense and interesting cover for old tree-stumps and rubble-heaps. . . ." I have seen it looking most effective on unimportant shrubs, its tangle of stems covered with small leaves of various shapes and spikes of small greenish-white flowers. The small leaves, thin and dull green, are roundish, heart-shaped, and fiddle-shaped; the flowers come in autumn.

In favourable districts, such as the Isle of Wight, the stems, which are wiry and much interlaced, usually go up to a height of 20 feet and retain their leaves till late winter. In some parts of New Zealand (its native habitat) the plants are evergreen and cover rocks with a thick mass of leaves and flowers.

This climber is often killed to ground level during the winter in gardens around London.

Mutisias come from the temperate and tropical parts of South America and are scarcely hardy enough for most districts in our country. In the south, however, like so many of our rare climbers they prosper and need no winter protection. But they seem to like walls; they grow taller there and bloom profusely and are truly flamboyant plants through the summer months. Only three or four different species are in cultivation here and about three are offered for sale by shrub specialists: *M. decurrens* seems to be the popular one.

Mutisias are evergreen and most of them attach themselves to the slender stems of bushes and low trees by leaf-tendrils: as in many climbers, the midrib of the leaf grows out into a tendril an inch or 2 or 3 inches long, which is often branched; as the stem grows and the leaves develop, so the tendrils that come from them pull it upward through the bush or the thick undergrowth to the sunlight.

The flowers love hot sunshine. They are composites, made up (as in the Daisy) of a centre (disc) of tiny flowers surrounded by large, showy ray-florets; they have been compared to the exotic Gazanias and the Marigolds (I have heard them called the Marigold Climbers).

Gardeners living in the south have the greatest success with them and it is worth going to see a well-grown specimen in full bloom.

M. clematis comes from the wild regions of the Andes of Colombia and Ecuador and will grow really well under cultivation if it can be given a mild climate, free from frosts and damp and a well-drained, light, sandy soil, which is kept loose by a good quantity of sharp rubble mixed in with it. It is advisable, too, to put some round the roots when planting the climber. It often takes several years to establish itself, but once it begins to grow freely, it will carry a profusion of orange-scarlet flowers from early summer to the autumn.

The plant is extremely vigorous and reaches a height of 20 or 30 feet, and more than that in a cool greenhouse, where it must be grown in districts near London. In Cornwall it is mostly planted on tallish shrubs like the *Leptospermum*, which do well there. But *M. clematis* has been known to grow so strong that it has weighed down the branches of *L. scoparium*, which have snapped and broken off during an autumn gale. It needs a more robust shrub than this to grow on: a tough, old apple-bush of no value would carry all the long, twisting stems without cracking.

Best of all is a porch on a south wall, which it will soon cover; a superfluity of long growths being well supported here and looking decorative hanging down over the front.

The young stems are slender and ribbed and covered, like other parts of the plant, with a thick, soft, whitish down. The evergreen leaves are pinnate and composed of from 6 to 10 leaflets, the largest measuring $1\frac{1}{2}$ inches long and $\frac{1}{2}$ inch wide. This species is a tendril-climber, like most of the genus; the tendrils, about 3 inches long, forked, growing from the ends of the main woolly leaf-stalks.

The flowers are very showy, of a brilliant orange-scarlet colour and measure $2\frac{1}{2}$ inches across; the ray-florets number about ten.

I have never seen this species outside of our warmest counties, except in a cool greenhouse near London, where it had soared up trellis to the roof and after a few years had to be pruned back to keep it in place. And this had to be done every December as it made a great deal of growth annually. There used to be a fine specimen of this climber in the Temperate House at Kew, where it blossomed from May to October.

The species, introduced in 1859, is very abundant on the slopes of Mt. Pichincha, not far from Quito, Ecuador.

M. decurrens (decurrent leaves), a native of Chile, is found in most shrub catalogues. Hillier's states: "Probably the most beautiful and hardiest of the Mutisias. . . . Favours partial shade. This species has withstood 26° of frost." Marchant says: "In the south and west it is much happier if planted in the open under some deciduous twiggy shrub and allowed to ramble at will."

It climbs by means of its tendrils, which spring from the apex of the leaves, and attains a height of 8 or 10 feet. Although the plant grows well on moderate-sized, twiggy shrubs in the open garden (Cornwall and south Devon are the best places for it), it flowers more freely when given a trellis on a west wall to climb up.

To provide the necessary shade for the roots, sink a few boulders in the soil (buried to two-thirds of their depth) round the plant. The soil should be a light loamy medium containing rubble. Where this Mutisia flourishes, it will carry hundreds of flowers during the season.

Its leaves are oblong, narrow, 3 to 5 inches long, about 1 inch wide, the base being extended down each side of the stem (decurrent). The flowers come singly on slender stalks and measure about 4 inches across. The disc flowers or florets are yellow; the ray-florets (about 15) a brilliant orange or vermilion colour.

This is a glorious climber for warm gardens near the sea; its flowers have been likened to large Marigolds or to single Dahlias. Richard Pearce discovered the plant and introduced it for Messrs. Veitch in 1859.

M. ilicifolia (holly-leaved) needs a cool greenhouse in districts near London, where it is sometimes grown in a large pot or a tub and given Beech twigs or slender bamboo canes to climb up. Outside it can be grown on twiggy shrubs or up a trellis on a west wall.

In its habitat, Chile, it will cover bushes 12 feet or more high with flower-heads 3 inches wide, which vary from pink to mauve and look very conspicuous against the dark green leathery leaves.

I have not seen many good specimens in any of our gardens. The best will be found in Cornwall; and there is a fine, mature plant in the rock-garden at the Botanic Gardens, Edinburgh.

This species was one of the first of the family to be introduced into Britain (1832) and has been mostly cultivated in conservatories and greenhouses.

The leaves are from 1 to 2½ inches long, the margins spiny-toothed, the midribs growing out into a tendril, which support the stem. The flower-heads, with their ray-florets, 8 to 12, measure about 3 inches across.

M. retusa, also from Chile, resembles the Holly-leaved Mutisia, but is apparently more amenable to cultivation. Its leaves, oblong-shaped, are about the same size as those of *M. ilicifolia*. The flower-heads, pink, come on stalks about 3 inches long – those of the other species are very short-stalked. A lovely climber for planting at the foot of a shrub, over which it will climb and reach a height of from 10 to 20 feet in favourable districts. The species was collected by Pearce for Messrs. Veitch in 1868.

This and the other species are usually propagated by cuttings of half-ripened wood, inserted in sand under glass and given gentle bottom heat.

The genus was named to commemorate J. C. Mutis, a Spanish botanist and student of the flora of South America (1732–1808).

Olearia erubescens is one of the evergreen 'Daisy Bushes' of Australasia and listed by most nurseries as tender and best grown against a warm wall or in a cool greenhouse. It belongs to the family of composites (as do the Mutisias); its flowers are made up of a centre of small yellow disc-florets and an outer ring of larger, white ray-florets.

The species has slender shoots, its loose habit making it suitable for growing against walls. It will go up to a height of 6 feet or so and look very attractive during May and June when it is covered with its daisy-like flowers. These are 1 inch wide, and made up of 6 to 8 yellow disc-florets and about 5 pure white ray-florets and are carried in a branched inflorescence. The flowers are charming against the evergreen leaves, which are a dark, glossy green above and a shining reddish-brown beneath; the largest 1½ inches in length and ¾ inch wide.

The 'Daisy Bushes' are most effective when they are massed in wide groups, though this particular species makes a fine specimen shrub against a low wall and a good one to grow in front of the early June-blooming Clematis 'La Lorraine', which has large satiny pink flowers suffused with lavender. Plant the Clematis on the opposite side of the wall and train its stems down the other side into the Olearia.

The genus is a large one, but very few species and varieties are seen in cultivation here: *O. virgata*, which has little floral beauty, but is attractive with its long, wire-like branches and small evergreen leaves (clothed with white felt underneath), is nearly always planted against a wall. In most of the shrubs, of course, it is their Aster-like flower-heads which are their great charm. The genus is closely related to the Aster family. The Olearias prefer a light, leafy soil, free from lime.

Pentstemon cordifolius (heart-shaped leaves) can only be grown in the open in gardens near London if it is planted against a sheltered south wall. It is frequently cut back by frosty weather in inland gardens, but sends up an abundance of new shoots the following spring. It is evergreen; its heart-shaped leaves (about 2 inches long) of a dark, glossy green colour are very pleasing against a wall during the winter months. But it is its flowers which are its chief delight. They are like those of the perennial Pentstemons which we grow in our herbaceous borders: tubular, two-lipped, the upper one hooded, the anthers are yellow, and the colour of the flowers in this species is rich scarlet. They come in large terminal panicles which are often 12 inches long and 9 inches wide; a magnificent show when they are carried freely. In the south they are in bloom from late June to the end of August and always much admired. Like most of the shrubby species of the genus, *P. cordifolius* is a native of California where it gets the hot sunshine it requires. The plant was discovered by David Douglas in 1831 and introduced into cultivation here about 1848. Our finest specimens are to be found in Cornwall where no doubt they get the optimum of sun. The plant thrives wonderfully in a light, well-drained soil, to which a little sifted leaf-mould has been added.

Periploca graeca (Grecian) is a hardy deciduous twining plant, which will go up to a height of 30 feet or more in our gardens. It is not a great beauty and, like several other climbers described in this chapter, it was cultivated in Britain during the sixteenth century. There weren't many ornamental climbers in cultivation at that time, and no doubt gardeners valued it greatly. Its flowers, about 1 inch wide, star-shaped, are brownish-purple inside and greenish-yellow on the outside and come in clusters of about twelve. The flowers have a peculiar heavy smell (deleterious if inhaled, some people say). The leaves ovalish, are from 2 to 4 inches in length and about half as wide. In autumn the plant carries narrow seed-pods containing seeds with a tuft of silky hairs at the end of them. Silk Vine is the common name of the plant.

This twiner does best on a wall but hardly seems good enough for one. (We can't compare it with any of the popular flowering climbers, for example.) But it does provide contrast when set among some of the large-flowered plants and is a foil to them. It looks charming draping a tall specimen of the prickly-leaved evergreen *Berberis darwinii*.

A native of South-east Europe (it is widely spread in Greece) the plant is obtainable from most nurseries and grows in any ordinary garden soil.

Phlomis fruticosa (shrubby) is the Jerusalem Sage. The name is well known to most gardeners, but the plant is actually rather rare. Like the twiner just described, it is a native of Southern Europe and has been cultivated in this country since the sixteenth century.

This grey, woolly-leaved shrub is on the tender side and often succumbs to frost when it is planted in gardens around London. However, I have grown two specimens on a low rockery-wall for many years in my garden (South Bucks.) and although they have been damaged by spells of cold weather, they have survived. A few stems lose their leaves, and these stems die back; but in the spring the plants begin to shoot out afresh and soon become bushy.

The leaves, 3 inches long, narrowish, hairy and velvety on both sides, are sage-coloured; and the flowers, a soft yellow, hood-shaped (like those of the Dead-nettle) are carried in clusters up the stems.

The specimens I grow face south-east, which is not perhaps

the best aspect for them: due south would have been better. Furthermore, they are in partial shade, which prevents them from blooming very freely. But the overhead sheltering branches of the trees have no doubt helped to preserve them. (See my comments on page 193 on growing this shrub in association with *Cistus* × *purpureus*.)

The Phlomis likes a light, sandy soil and seems to tolerate drought. It is easily propagated by cuttings: I have rooted them in the garden.

Pileostegia viburnoides. An evergreen climber, introduced by Wilson from China in 1908. It is also found in the Khasia Hills, India, and in Formosa. In its habitat it grows up trees or along rocky ground, clinging to surfaces with its strong aerial roots. It will attain a height of 20 feet in favourable places and seems to do best in partial shade. When it thrives, as it will on a shady wall, it is magnificent with its panicles of white flower-heads, set off by the narrow, leathery, evergreen leaves. Like the self-clinging Hydrangeas, to which it is related, it needs an enormous amount of space. It would be difficult to find a suitable place for it in a small garden.

The leaves are from 2 to 6 inches long and about half as wide, a dark, dull green; the flowers densely packed in terminal panicles, 4 inches wide and as high. The numerous stamens to the individual flowers give the panicles a pretty, lacy appearance.

This evergreen climber blooms late (it is often at its best during the last week in September), thus it is doubly valuable in gardens where room can be found for it to spread itself out well.

It flourishes on a wall at Kew and seems to be completely hardy there. A rich, deep-cultivated soil suits it best. Marchant describes it as: "A handsome shrub with large, glossy, laurel-like leaves, for a semi-shady position." Twenty years ago a plant cost half a crown. The specific epithet *viburnoides* refers to the shape of the flowers.

Prunus triloba plena is like the Kerria in one respect: it is a hardy deciduous flowering shrub that is nearly always grown against a sunny wall. Some growers, however, regard it as being on the tender side; Marchant says it is not hardy enough for general planting in the open. It often fails to give a good show in borders in gardens near London; gardeners who know the shrub always give it a wall. Seen in full bloom for the first time, it is startling in the beauty and profusion of its blossom. All the plants I know have been grown against walls 10 feet or so high, the shrubs reaching to the top and spreading out wider than they are tall, the lowest branches, pendent and touching the ground, and the others standing out 2 or 3 feet from the wall, all covered from top to the base with rosette-shaped, rose-coloured flowers; they come so thick on the branches that no foliage is visible. (I have not yet come across any plants that grew in the open garden, though there are said to be good flowering bushes in shrubberies round the south coast.)

The shrub is full of blossom at the end of March, but the flowers are seldom damaged by frosts when it has a wall behind it. Its leaves are ovalish, about 2 inches long; the flowers 1½ inches across, very double, and of an exquisite rose shade.

An annual pruning is necessary: the shrubs are cut back close as soon as the blossom has fallen; they then shoot out during the summer and flower as freely the following year.

This Prunus needs a deep, loamy soil and doesn't mind lime. It is easily increased by layering some of the lowest branches; or cuttings of firm wood may be taken in July.

When buying a shrub, a specimen on its own roots should be asked for: those grafted on Plum-stock are troublesome because of the suckers thrown up. The species *P. triloba* is a native of China; and our double form was introduced from Chinese gardens by Robert Fortune in 1855. These Prunus belong to the Almond (*Amygdalus*) section of the genus. The double-flowered shrub is used for forcing into blossom during the winter; if grown in a pot under glass, it can be had in full bloom by February.

Pueraria thunbergiana is listed by most nurserymen who sell it as a half-hardy climber. It is rarely seen in our gardens and seldom flourishes in our climate. The plant grows luxuriantly in the South of France, where it goes up to a height of 20 feet or more and is used to cover summer-houses, arbours and the like. Mostly, the long stems die back in winter when the plant is grown in colder regions. The fragrant, purplish flowers are seldom seen here. They are pea-shaped, ½ inch long, and come in racemes 10 inches in length and bloom in August. The seed-pods, 4 inches long, covered with greyish-brown hairs, are freely borne on plants in the south; and from them, new plants are easily raised every year. (They should be sown in pots in a greenhouse and the seedlings planted out in a good, rich loam about May – they grow rapidly in warm, sheltered parts of Cornwall and Devon.) The leaves are composed of 3 leaflets, the middle one 6 inches long, diamond-shaped, the others are smaller and ovalish.

Few climbers grow so quickly as this plant; it is a native of China and Japan and is known as the Kudzu Vine. The genus was named in honour of M. N. Puerari (1765–1845), Professor at Copenhagen.

Punica granatum (*Punica* is from *Puniceus*, Punic, Carthaginian: *Malum punicum*, "Apple of Carthage", being an early name of the pomegranate. *Granatum* is the Latin name of the fruit, with its numerous fleshy seeds).

This flowering Pomegranate is tender in gardens near London and needs to be grown in front of a south wall. Farther south, where it would be safer, it is nevertheless grown in the same way and may there bear fruits. Bean in *Trees and Shrubs Hardy in the British Isles* mentions a tree that covered the whole of the front of a house at Bath and during one season bore a large quantity of fruit. The species does not usually fruit in our climate. But we grow it (and two or three varieties of it) specifically for the glorious scarlet flowers. These come from June to September; they are tubular, with 5 or more crumpled petals; when fully open each flower measures about $1\frac{1}{2}$ inches across. The leaves, deciduous, are narrow, a bright shining green, the largest 3 inches in length: a fine foil to the brilliant scarlet blossom.

Those who have seen it full of flower in cold greenhouses near London, have been seized with the desire to grow it in their gardens – not having a greenhouse. Can they grow it outside in the London district? I believe I have seen a variety of it, not in flower, planted on a wall of the Temperate House at Kew. But I have never seen any good flowering specimens in inland gardens. I advise those who are greatly attracted by it to try the dwarf variety *P. granatum* var. *nana* in a pot and house it through the winter months. It seldom goes above 2 feet in height and is amenable to pot-culture: a favourite pot-plant in France and Italy. Give it a rich, well-drained loamy soil and feed it often with doses of weak liquid manure as soon as the flower-buds begin to show. The colour is as vivid as that of the flowers of the type plant.

However, it has proved successful in gardens south of London, when it has been planted close to the wall of a house and given adequate protection from December to April. (I have seen wire-netting rigged up on stout stakes, fixed at intervals round the front and the sides of the plant, the space between the shrub and the wire being filled with bracken and straw, but the top left open to the air.)

The actual *P. granatum* is not so often grown as the double-flowered *P. granatum* var. *plena*, whose flowers look even more fiery-red than those of the single-flowered plants. It needs the same sort of soil (rich loam) and the same situation.

In the wild *P. granatum* makes a small tree up to 25 feet in height (its habitat is thought to be Persia and North-west India.) It has been cultivated in Britain since the sixteenth century.

The variety *nana* grows taller in the south; it may reach a height of about 6 feet; and where it prospers, it makes a magnificent free-flowering hedge. In gardens in regions on the Pacific seaboard, as far north as San Francisco, this glowing red-flowered bush arrests the attention from a long way off. When grown under glass, the shrub often blooms right through the winter.

Most shrub specialists have a selection of the Pomegranate shrubs.

Pyracantha. (The name is from *pyr*, fire; and *acanthos*, thorn: the fire-thorn.) The flame-coloured or scarlet berries cover the plants when they are grown close against walls. There are about half a dozen species, evergreen, hardy enough for most districts but bear a profusion of fruits only when the plants are grown against warm walls. Three are well-known and obtainable from most shrub nurseries. The first, *P. coccinea* (scarlet) is the most popular and will be seen growing up the front of a house (perhaps two specimens forming an archway over a door) and green all through the spring; in June the small white flowers come and these are followed by round berries which transform the plant into a glowing mass of scarlet.

The long season through which the berries remain scarlet makes these shrubs doubly valuable. Some are covered for fully six months, provided the birds don't get them. It is worth netting the shrubs to frighten them away.

This species, with its thorny shoots and small narrowish leaves (the biggest about 2 inches long) will go up to a height of 15 feet in the open and more than that on a wall. Good berrying specimens, round in shape, may be seen in many gardens. They make successful ornamental specimen shrubs for lawns during the autumn and the winter. But it is as a wall shrub that we value this and the other species.

The variety *P. coccinea* var. *Lalandel* (raised from seed by M. Lalande of Angers in 1874) is said to be hardier. It is more vigorous and has wider leaves and berries of an orange colour. The shrub appears in most catalogues. *P. coccinea*, a native of Southern Europe and Asia Minor, was introduced into Britain as long ago as 1629.

P. crenato-serrata often appears in shrub lists as *P. yunnanensis*. It is a native of Yunnan, China, from where it was introduced by Father Ducloux in 1906. This species, closely related to the others, may be distinguished by its leaves which have broad, rounded ends – the leaves of the Pyracantha are mostly tapered. It makes a good evergreen wall shrub up to 12 or 18 feet high and bears an abundance of orange-shaped berries, which colour rather late and remain on the shoots often as late as March.

P. rogersiana is the least vigorous of the species mentioned here and thus suitable for limited spaces, say, the wall of a cottage. It can, of course, be clipped into shape. (Clipping should be done, when it is thought necessary, immediately after the berries have fallen, but any drastic cutting back will mean the loss of flowers and berries for a season.) The plant seldom goes above a height of 10 feet and has small leaves, narrowish and tapering to the base. The fruits are very abundant, round and of a yellow-orange shade and remain on the branches almost till the spring. The small white flowers, which come in June, are attractive and completely cover the plant. In the variety *semi-plena* the numerous petals make the flowers even more conspicuous – the plant is beautiful both in blossom and in fruit.

Several varieties are offered for sale by nurseries. Var. *aurantiaca* has orange-yellow berries; var. *flava*, bright yellow.

P. rogersiana, a native of Yunnan, was discovered by Delavay in 1889 and introduced by Forrest in 1911. The first plants exhibited in England were shown at the R.H.S. Show in March, 1913, by Mr. Coltman-Rogers, for whom the plant was named.

The Pyracantha thrive in any ordinary loamy soil and need a sunny position; they are increased by seeds or by cuttings of ripened wood taken in July.

Rhaphithamnus cyanocarpus (blue berries) is another plant from the hot climate of Chile and needing, as most of them do, rather special treatment in our country. People living in Cornwall and Devon and other warm parts are fortunate in being able to grow it and its tender companions successfully. This plant is an evergreen shrub or small tree which must have the protection of a wall in inland gardens. Many shrub specialists offer it for sale and state that it is a pretty wall shrub suitable for mild climates. Hillier notes that it has attained tree-like size in a sheltered mid-Sussex garden. In its habitat it makes a tree 25 feet or so high and is there very striking when in fruit. Its leaves are a very dark green above, paler beneath, the largest about ¾ inch long and ½ inch wide; they are broadly ovalish in shape and attractive all through the winter months. The flowers are small, tubular and come singly or in pairs in the leaf-axils. They are pale blue and quite pretty in April. But the great attraction of this wall shrub is the fruit, which comes in late summer – berries about ½ inch wide of a bright, lovely blue colour. They are borne abundantly on plants which are growing well in warm sunny places and give a wonderful show of colour. Berries and fruits of this particular shade are extremely rare. The shrub is certainly worth a trial against a warm wall in inland gardens. It likes a deep, loamy soil and full sun. It may be seen against a wall at Kew. W. Lobb introduced the species about 1843. The generic name is from *rhapis*, a needle; and *thamnos*, a shrub; it refers to the spiny character of some of the species.

Rhus toxicodendron var. *radicans* is the Poison Ivy, a climbing form of the deciduous shrub, which is bushy and about 8 feet tall. Both the typical plant and the climber have good autumn-tinting leaves. They are a glowing red and orange in October and November. The plant ascends walls by means of its aerial roots and in such a position displays its coloured leaves to best advantage. These are composed of three leaflets, the terminal one being the largest – from 2 to 5 inches long. The flowers, small and a dull white, come in slender panicles 2 inches in length and are followed by small, whitish berries. This climbing Rhus is worth growing because it is a self-clinging plant and has such striking autumnal colours, but one should be careful how one handles it. The yellow milky juice which comes from the stem when it is cut will blister the skin. Taking cuttings is a risk for people with sensitive skins; they should wear gloves when handling the plant. It is seldom listed in catalogues, which is just as well. The Poison Ivy, a native of the eastern United States, was in cultivation in England during the seventeenth century.

Rubus is the family of Brambles, some of which, with their long, coloured stems and attractive leaves, are valuable ornamental climbers for the winter months. They are most at home in the wild garden, but I have seen several planted in conjunction with climbers on walls and they have not looked out of place.

R. australis and one or two varieties described under this name thrive best in such a place, for they are rather tender in our climate. This species, a native of New Zealand, is a climbing evergreen shrub which makes its way to the top of tall trees in the wild. The zig-zagged stems have small hooked prickles. The leaves are extremely variable. In the form called var. *pauperatus*, the leaflets are almost reduced to midribs, which are furnished with prickly spines. With the help of these spines (on leaves and stems) the plant climbs and makes inextricable tangles on trees and shrubs.

R. flagelliflorus is a native of Central and Western China, where it grows at altitudes up to 6,000 feet. It is a climbing, evergreen shrub like the preceding and is hardier than that species and its varieties. Gardeners who grow it usually train it on a long pole or a stake about 10 feet tall, and it is then very graceful and decorative with its large dark green sharply-toothed leaves (the underside yellow-felted) and its long stems covered with a whitish felt. The stems grow as much as 6 feet in a season. This ornamental Bramble does best in partial shade and may be seen trailing over banks in some gardens; in shade the leaves take on an attractive marbled appearance. The flowers, insignificant, are white, the fruits, shining black and edible.

R. henryi bambusarum is another evergreen Chinese species and grows abundantly in woodlands and thickets in mountainous regions up to 7,000 feet. Its leaves are usually made up of 3 narrow leaflets, each from 2 to 5 inches long, pointed, dark green above and white beneath. Pink flowers, insignificant; fruits, black and good to eat. The long cordlike stems go up to a height of 20 feet; they are covered with a white cobweb-like substance which later turns dark green, and push their way up through twiggy shrubs and trail downwards effectively. The full beauty and elegance of this climbing plant is best revealed when it is grown up a pole; the stems are tied into position round it, then when they are sufficiently long, they arch and hang symmetrically round it. The species, first discovered by Henry in Hupeh, was introduced into cultivation by Wilson in 1900.

R. laciniatus is commonly known as the cut-leaved Bramble; the leaves are composed of about 5 leaflets, deeply divided, arranged round the stalk. It is a deciduous, scandent shrub, which may be seen in many of our gardens, where it is usually trained up trellis or strong wire-netting. It is also seen on fences at the end of gardens. Its foliage is attractive through the spring and the early summer: so much so that some gardeners train it on the uprights of a pergola – the stems attain a height of 8 feet or so.

Normally it is grown for its clusters of large fruits, which are black, sweet and delicious when ripe.

The origin of the plant is uncertain; it has become naturalized in North America and is thought to be indigenous to Britain. Mature, well-grown specimens have large, handsome leaves, often 9 inches long.

In warm climates the lower stems become as thick as one's wrist and the leaves are practically evergreen.

R. lineatus is a deciduous or semi-evergreen rambling plant which prospers only in our warm, southern gardens, where it will attain a height of 10 feet and display its beautiful foliage when the stems are trained on trellis. The leaves are composed of usually 5 radiating leaflets; above they are a dark green and underneath covered with an exquisite silvery down; the numerous parallel veins (sometimes as many as 50 pairs on one leaflet) add to the beauty of the foliage. The flowers are small and white; the fruits red or yellow. This uncommon species is a native of the Sikkim Himalaya, South-west China and Malaya. It is very abundant in Yunnan, China, where Forrest collected it in 1905.

There are 3 shrubby species which are offered for sale by nurseries and prized by gardeners for some distinctive feature: in *R. biflorus* and *R. cockburnianus* it is the whitewashed effect of the slender stems, so conspicuous through the winter months. I have seen both planted against a wall and looking startlingly white and artificial on a grey winter day. *R. biflorus*, from the Himalaya, has stems 1 inch thick and 10 feet tall covered with a white waxy coating. It should be planted in a deep, rich loam, which causes the stems to grow thicker and whiter. *R. cockburnianus* should be similarly treated. It is considered to be the best of the 'whitewashed' Brambles.

R. deliciosus is noted for its flowers; it is the loveliest of all that have flowers worth looking at; and I have seen the plant trained against a low wall, covering a large portion with interlacing, thornless stems carrying pure white single flowers 2 inches wide, as lovely as Wild Roses.

The species, a native of the Rocky Mountains, was discovered in 1820 by Dr. James and introduced to Britain 50 years later.

All the Rubi like a good loamy soil, and should have old wood and weak stems cut out. They can be propagated by seed, layering or by root division.

Two species of *Sabia* are grown in our gardens and are valued for their blue fruits: they have small, insignificant flowers. *Sabia latifolia* is a deciduous climbing shrub up to 10 feet tall, which does best in partial shade. It is rarely seen; no doubt because it has little floral beauty, but it is worth growing for its fruits, which are very decorative in the autumn. The leaves are ovalish, and the flowers, small, somewhat globose in shape, come in clusters of 3, and are first greenish-yellow, then reddish-brown. I have seen the plant at Kew, growing in the open and in gardens farther south, where it was usually trained up trellis on a wall, along with other climbers.

A native of West China, it was discovered by Pratt in 1888 and introduced into cultivation by Wilson in 1908. I have not seen the plant or the following species listed in any catalogues.

S. schumanniana, also a native of West China, was introduced by Wilson the same year. It is similar to *S. latifolia*, reaches the same height, but has smaller and narrower leaves and longer flower-stalks. The flowers are greenish or a purplish colour and rounded in shape. Like those of the other species, they bloom in May. The kidney-shaped fruits turn blue-black in October and are striking when they are borne in quantity. Both climbers are hardy and thrive in any ordinary garden soil.

Sargentodoxa cuneata is a deciduous climber as rare as the two species of Sabia. It is a twiner which reaches a height of 25 feet or more and has dark, glossy green leaves composed of 3 leaflets and pendulous racemes of small greenish-yellow fragrant flowers. The flowers are unisexual, the female type bearing purplish-blue berries about ¼ inch wide in October. The plant is attractive in flower in May and thought to need the protection of a wall if it is to survive our winter weather.

It is botanically distinct from any other plant in cultivation: there is no other species, and the genus and the Natural Order *Sargentodoxaceae* were founded for it. A native of Central China, where it was collected by Henry in 1887, and later by Wilson, who introduced it in 1907. The plant was named in honour of Professor C. S. Sargent, the founder of the Arnold Arboretum.

Schizandra. Several species of this genus may be obtained from shrub nurseries. Most shrub specialists have the ones described below. These are hardy, twining by habit and climb trees; in this country, however, they seem to do best on shady or semi-shady walls; and in such a position must be trained on trellis-work.

They are for the most part aromatic; some deciduous, some evergreen and related to the Magnolias. We grow them chiefly for their handsome leaves and the scarlet or orange berries.

S. chinensis, a native of China and Japan, was introduced in 1860 and may be seen in many of our southern gardens, where on west or north walls it has grown up tall, spreading its branches out fully to 20 feet or more. The young stems are red; the leaves (deciduous) ovalish, from 2 to 4 inches long; and the flowers, ½ inch wide, a pale rose colour and fragrant, come in clusters on pendulous stalks; they bloom in April and May and are followed by scarlet berries ¼ inch wide on a stalk 4 inches long. The dried wood has a pleasant, spicy smell.

S. henryi, deciduous like the above species, and twining round shrubs and trees in its habitat (China): it is common in Western Hupeh and Szechwan. It has bright green leaves which are glaucous beneath, ovalish in shape, 3 to 4 inches long; the flowers, white, unisexual, measure ½ inch across, and come on stout 3-inch stalks. The bright red berries are borne on spikes about 2 inches in length and are apparently much relished by the Chinese. The species is easily distinguished from the preceding by the triangular shape of its young branches and its shining, thicker leaves. *S. henryi* is quite hardy in the London district; I have seen it in the autumn growing up tall, open shrubs and covered with quantities of bright red fruits. As a flowering climber in April and May it is also very attractive.

Wilson collected the plant in 1900 for Messrs. Veitch, but it had been previously discovered by Henry much earlier.

S. rubriflora (red-flowered), sometimes described as *S. grandiflora rubriflora,* is handsome in flower, the buds especially attracting one by their deep crimson colour: they hang down like clusters of cherries on red stalks; when fully open, they measure 1 inch across. They bloom in April and May, and the red berries, closely packed on stems 3 to 6 inches long, appear in September. Both the flowers and the berries look very bright against the green leaves, the largest of which are 5 inches long and about half as wide. Some plants are grown on shady walls where they prosper and seem to bloom more freely than anywhere else, though some also do well when trained up poles or over upright stout branches stuck in the ground – particularly in a shady place. Marchant describes the plant as "fast-growing and interesting during April and May with its ¾-inch red flowers. Its fruits are bright red."

A fruiting specimen was given an Award of Merit by the Royal Horticultural Society in September, 1925. The species, native to West Szechwan, where it was discovered on Mt. Omei by E. Faber in 1887, was introduced by Wilson in 1908.

Marchant also lists *S. sphenanthera,* a vigorous climber, "and attractive during April and May with numerous coppery-yellow flowers." Its best season is the autumn, when it bears clusters of scarlet berries closely packed on stalks 6 to 8 inches long. They stand out well against the green leaves, ovalish or roundish, from 2 to 4 inches long. The species, native to Hupeh and Szechwan, was introduced by Wilson in 1907.

Most of the plants that I have seen in cultivation in this country were growing in a deep, moist soil and were thriving remarkably. None was in full sun; most of them grew on walls. Propagation is by cuttings of half-ripened wood in a gentle bottom heat.

Schizophragma. Two species of deciduous climbing plants (sometimes called Climbing Hydrangeas) which support their stems by aerial roots like a number of other climbers we have mentioned. Both species are grown in our gardens and can be got from most shrub specialists.

S. hydrangeoides comes from Japan and goes up to a height of 40 feet in favourable places. It has deep green, very coarsely-toothed leaves, ovalish, 4 to 6 inches long and half as wide; paler and rather glaucous beneath. Its flowers are small, slightly fragrant, yellowish-white and come in a flattish inflorescence about 8 to 10 inches across, and each section terminates in a heart-shaped bract (an enlarged sepal) $1\frac{1}{2}$ inches long, which makes the inflorescence an uncommonly beautiful one. The climber shows off its flowers to best advantage when it is planted on a wall. I have seen it on tall trees, but much of its beauty was lost among the thick branches and foliage. In its habitat it grows in this way and is often found in company with *Hydrangea petiolaris*, with which *S. hydrangeoides* is often confused. The latter is easily distinguished from the Hydrangea by the single large bract at the end of each section of the inflorescence. It blooms from July to October and is a picturesque, giant-size climber for large gardens.

S. integrifolia (undivided leaves). A specimen exhibited in June, 1936, at a Royal Horticultural Society's Show received an Award of Merit. The species is distinguished from the other by its leaves, which are usually entire; they are from 3 to 7 inches long, slenderly pointed and greyish-green beneath. The inflorescence, 9 to 12 inches across, is more showy than that in the other plant, the bracts terminating the sections being larger, sometimes $3\frac{1}{2}$ inches long and narrowly ovate. Dr. Rehder states that the plant is less hardy in the U.S.A. than *S. hydrangeoides*. Both species flourish more luxuriantly in our southern gardens than they do north of London. They like partial shade in the south and need, wherever they are grown, a good, loamy soil which must never be allowed to dry out.

S. integrifolia, a native of Central China, where it often climbs up sheer cliff, was introduced by Wilson in 1901.

These plants are easily propagated by cuttings or by layering the lower stems. Hillier has both species and also the variety *S. integrifolia molle* (soft); the word refers to the downy nature of the leaves and their stalks.

Senecio scandens is also listed by Hillier and described in a pre-war catalogue as a "Recently introduced scandent shrub from West China, stated to exceed 15 feet. The yellow, daisy-like flowers form large terminal panicles."

In the wild it scrambles over shrubs and gives a bright display of yellow flowers in the autumn. The leaves are ovalish and toothed and measure from 2 to 4 inches long; and the flowers, like yellow daisies (¾ inch wide), come in wide, terminal panicles. Gardeners who grow it state that it needs a south wall and should be trained up trellis-work. In the warm climate of Cornwall and the Channel Islands, however, it is a good, semi-climbing shrub to plant against uninteresting shrubs. It comes into bloom in late summer and thrives in any ordinary garden soil.

Sinofranchetia chinensis. The genus was named in memory of Adrien René Franchet, the French botanist, who did much valuable research work in China. He died in 1900. The plant is a tall-growing deciduous twiner, reaching to the top of trees 40 feet high in its habitat: Central and West China. The main stem on well-grown plants is often 4 inches thick; the leaves, composed of 3 leaflets, come on purplish stems, the leaflets being from 3 to 6 inches long, and glaucous beneath. The flowers are not interesting: they are small, inconspicuous and a dull white; but the fruits, blue-purple and the size of a grape, are very ornamental in the autumn when they are produced in quantity.

This evergreen climber is not difficult to grow, but only gardeners with plenty of room to spare will want it. Its foliage is handsome all through the summer; the plant looks best twining round a tall shrub on the edge of a woodland.

It is related to *Akebia*, *Holboellia*, etc., and has been found growing at altitudes up to 17,000 feet in mountainous regions in Western China. Wilson introduced the plant in 1907.

Sinomenium acutum is another vigorous deciduous twining

plant, as little known probably as the *Sinofranchetia*. It is a
native, too, of Central and Western China, and also of Japan,
where it has been in cultivation for many years. In nature it
climbs up trees to a height of 20 feet or so, twining round thin
branches with its bright green, slender stems. The leaves are
extremely variable: they may be heart-shaped or divided, 3- or
5-lobed, or kidney-shaped. They are a bright green colour and
measure from 2 to 6 inches long and 1 to 4 inches wide. The
flowers are small and insignificant, yellow, and come in slender
panicles about 10 inches long. It is for the fruits, blue-black
round berries, that we grow the plant. As the flowers are unisexual, it is necessary to grow the male and the female plants
together if fruits are wanted.

Wilson introduced this rare climber from China for Messrs.
Veitch of Exeter in 1901. It is perfectly hardy and succeeds in
any ordinary garden soil.

Smilax. The name is familiar to most people, for the foliage
plant much used for indoor decorations, bouquets, etc., is commonly called Smilax (the Smilax of florists); but this is actually
an Asparagus, *A. medeoloides*, grown in greenhouses and
trained on wires or strings, so that it is readily cut for use. A
genuine Smilax, *S. lanceolata* (the Florida Smilax) is tender,
usually grown in a cool greenhouse, and widely used in the
trade.

The species we grow in this country are climbing plants
which ascend by means of tendrils. These are the stipulary
type, two of which come from the base of the leaf-stalk or the
sheath. They are produced all the way up the stem and as soon
as they are extended and have touched a suitable support, they
grasp it and then contract, forming an elongated coil. Thus, as
with the other tendril climbers, the plant is held securely to its
support, the coiled tendril enabling the plant to sway outwards
when moved by the wind. (See Fig. 14.)

Our first, *S. aspera*, is the most attractive but can be grown
out of doors only in the warmest parts of the British Isles. It
grows 8 to 10 feet high, its stems being spiny and its leaves
(evergreen) varying in shape. They are mostly arrow- or
heart-shaped at the base in cultivated plants and measure $1\frac{1}{2}$
inches to 4 inches long; the margins are prickly. The fragrant,
greenish-white flowers are carried in graceful racemes about

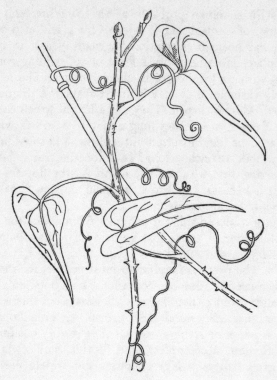

Figure 14.

The stipular tendrils of the Common smilax
(*Smilax aspera*).

4 inches long during August and September; and the red berries
are about the size of a pea.

There are two varieties: var. *maculata*, with leaves marbled
with white; and var. *mauritanica*, which has larger leaves and
is not so spiny.

In the south of England this Smilax is often allowed to ramble
freely over old tree stumps and there it looks very picturesque,
but in such an open position it may be badly damaged by frost.
It is safer against a warm wall. In a cool greenhouse, where
perhaps it is mostly grown, it flourishes luxuriantly and makes a
beautiful climbing foliage plant.

The species is native to Southern Europe – often seen in the
regions of the Mediterranean – North Africa and the Canary

Islands, and has been cultivated in England since the middle of the seventeenth century.

S. excelsa (very tall). I have seen it grown against a wall in southern districts, but it made a thicket of stems suckering far out into other climbers growing near. Most of the Smilaxes throw up these underground shoots and are consequently troublesome. They are best planted near old trees and shrubs in sheltered parts of the garden. This species will reach the tops of tall trees and look very attractive with its broadly ovalish leaves, which in the south persist till a severe frost comes: they are evergreen in hot climates. The flowers are carried in umbels, and the fruits are red. This Smilax, a native of South-east Europe and Asia Minor, was introduced in 1739.

S. glauca is a deciduous or evergreen climber, delightfully glaucous in its leaves and its berries: a tall climbing species which is mostly seen in wild gardens and growing luxuriantly on trees. Hillier lists it and states that sometimes the whole plant is glaucous. The species is figured in Vol. 43 (t., 1846) of the *Botanical Magazine*. The plant is a male. "It is hardy and of easy culture. . . ." The plate shows a single stem standing up from a horizontal branch which is sparsely furnished with small, pinkish white thorns. The glaucous green of the undersides of the deeply veined leaves shows up well; the tiny, lobed flowers are greenish-white, quite insignificant and come in pairs as do the tendrils from the base of the leaf-stalks. *S. glauca* was introduced from North America about 1826.

S. hispida (bristly), a native of Central North America and Ontario, is one of the hardiest species and one of the few which does not sucker. It is a slow-growing plant which never spreads far but climbs high into trees up to 50 feet. The lower stems are furnished with slender spines and bristles, the upper parts practically unarmed. The leaves are often heart-shaped, from 2 to 6 inches long, deciduous; the flowers, greenish-yellow, are followed by small round, blue-black berries in autumn. By keeping the plant neatly pruned, it will make an excellent hedge. Two common names of this species are Bamboo Brier and Hay Brier.

S. megalantha is the handsomest and best of the Smilaxes for foliage effects. The leaves are very variable in shape and size, from 3 to 9 inches long and about 1 inch to 6 inches wide, leathery and a dark, glossy green above, glaucous beneath. The flowers, greenish in colour, are followed by coral-red fruits, $\frac{1}{2}$ inch in diameter, and are very showy in the autumn. A native of Hupeh, West Szechwan, and Yunnan, China, and introduced by Wilson in 1907.

S. rotundifolia. Some gardeners condemn it as a rank, weedy vine, spreading by underground rhizomes all over the place. Hillier's list it in their catalogue: " 'Common Green Brier' or 'Horse Brier'. A very hardy species with prickly stems and broadly heart-shaped leaves." It is best planted in a woodland-garden or near a tall group of shrubs (of no great ornamental value) and allowed to climb freely as it does in its habitat (North America), where it reaches a height of 30 or 40 feet. It looks particularly fine on the white-stemmed Birch (*Betula pendula*) and is vigorous enough to reach from one tree to another. The leaves are oval-shaped or sometimes roundish (deciduous: evergreen in warm districts) and smooth and a glossy green on both sides. The small greenish-yellow flowers come in June and the fruits are black berries with a glaucous bloom. The species, introduced here in 1760, is the commonest and most vigorous of the Smilaxes we grow. They prosper in any ordinary soil and are easily propagated by root-division.

Solanum. Two species are occasionally seen in our gardens and both are more successful in the warmer regions of the south than near London. The first, *S. crispum*, must be grown against a warm wall in inland gardens and there will go up to a height of 15 feet or so – in the south and the south-west of England it is much taller. It is a scandent shrub and often needs supporting when planted close to a wall: wires stretched across in front of it will keep the stems tidy. The leaves, semi-evergreen, are ovalish, from 2 to 5 inches long and downy on both sides. The flowers, blue-purple with a yellow centre, come in long-stalked clusters, 3 to 6 inches across; they are fragrant and bloom from June to September. Each flower is about $1\frac{1}{2}$ inches wide. In warm, maritime gardens the plant may be grown in an open border and, by pruning back the long annual growths, kept to a well-shaped bush up to 15 or 20 feet tall. It fruits freely in the south, the berries being the size of a pea and yellowish-white in colour. There is a variety called *autum-*

nalis[1] or the 'Glasneven Variety' which is not so hardy as the type; it has deeper purplish flowers and blooms rather later. Both plants succeed in quite thin, sandy soils. The species, a native of Chile, was introduced in 1830.

S. jasminoides is the other species, an evergreen climber from Brazil. Its common name is the Potato Vine (*Solanum* is the Potato Family) and it climbs by means of its twining stems. It is more tender than *S. crispum* and hardly a success near London. In the south it is usually grown on a wall, where it spreads out and soon covers a large area with its grey-blue flowers and thin, glossy green leaves, which are from 1 to 3 inches long. The flowers come in loose clusters and bloom from July till the frosts nip them.

Most people who can grow these plants prefer the white-flowered form of this species, viz. var. *album*, which carries a profusion of white flowers with a yellow centre. A more picturesque climber, I think, than the type plant. Both prosper in ordinary garden soil and are propagated by cuttings.

Sollya is a small genus comprising 2 species of evergreen twiners, viz. *S. fusiformis* (it is now usually referred to a *S. heterophylla*); and *S. parviflora*. They are natives of Australia and flourish in the warm, dry climate of that country. With us they need a cool greenhouse or a wall in our southern and south-western maritime gardens. Gardeners have tried them on south walls in their gardens near London; the plants have lived for several years and flowered, but they had to be partly covered up during severe frosts.

Whether they are grown out of doors or in a greenhouse, they need a well-drained, peaty soil and must be given some sort of support: trellis or wires are recommended by people who grow them.

S. heterophylla (variously-shaped leaves) is known as the 'Bluebell Creeper' of Australia and is a very lovely, tall, spreading twiner, suitable for the front of a house in such districts as South Devon and Cornwall. Mr. Ernest Markham, F.R.H.S., an authority on climbing plants, mentions a specimen which grew in a garden near Truro, Cornwall. It clothed the whole side of a house, many feet in height, with nodding blue flowers.

[1] A fine specimen grows on a wall at the Savill Gardens, Windsor; the branches are trained out on horizontal wires.

The leaves are sometimes broadly-ovalish, sometimes narrow, usually 1½ to 3 inches long. In early June the cup-shaped flowers open and continue to bloom till late August; they are about ½ inch wide, of a lovely blue colour, and come in nodding clusters of 5 and often twice that number. The species was introduced into England in 1830, but its tenderness has made it a rarity. In the variety *angustifolus* the leaves are narrower and the stem less twining. I have not seen this variety listed in catalogues. Marchant and Hillier offer the type plant. It may still be possible to get the other species, *S. parviflora* (I have seen it described in old catalogues under the name of *S. drummondii* – quoted now only as a synonym). Its flowers are not so showy as those of *S. heterophylla*, and its leaves are smaller; nonetheless it is a very beautiful blue-flowered climbing plant and certainly worth a trial on a warm wall in a sheltered garden. It is more twining in habit than the other species. Its habitat is the Swan River region near Brodie Plains, New South Wales. The best place for this slender, twining, hare-bell climber in inland gardens is a cool greenhouse. It does well in a pot of rich, peaty soil and will climb up bamboo supports.

The plants are propagated by cuttings of fairly firm shoots, which must be inserted in sand under glass.

The genus was named in honour of the English botanist R. H. Solly, 1778–1858. Both species are closely related to *Billardiera.* See page 109 for the evergreen species from Tasmania, *B. longiflora.*

Sophora. (The name is from *sophera*, an Arabic word for a tree with pea-shaped flowers.) There are two sections of the genus: *Sophora* proper, with pea-shaped flowers; and *Edwardsia*, in which the flowers are larger and tubular-shaped. Plants belonging to both sections are in cultivation here; but most of them are on the tender side and should be grown on walls. I have never seen the best known, viz. *S. tetraptera* and its varieties grown anywhere else in inland gardens. In warm, southern climates it grows into a tall shrub or small tree in the open garden and needs no protection. This species (the specific epithet means four-winged) is native to both Chile and New Zealand, habitats remarkably wide apart. The seed-pods, from 2 to 8 inches long, have four thin ridges or wings running lengthwise and are noticeably constricted between each seed, which gives the longer pods a peculiar, necklace-like shape.

I have seen this species growing well in the open in nursery gardens near Bournemouth. One, on a wall, was nearly 20 feet tall, and retained its leaves till late December. These were fern-like, made up of leaflets about ¼ inch long, probably 50 on the stalk. Its golden-yellow flowers opened in May and were carried in pendulous racemes, the foliage a delightful foil to them. Each flower tubular-shaped and about 1 inch long. Another specimen grew in a cold greenhouse, where it was evergreen and flowered earlier than the outdoor plant. Near by on a west wall grew the variety *microphylla*, which has smaller, more numerous leaves and flowers, but an equally beautiful wall-shrub. It grew 15 feet high. Both these plants were introduced from New Zealand in 1772. They have not proved hardy enough for gardens near London, even when they have been grown on a wall. A fairly light sandy soil is best for them.

S. macrocarpa (large-fruited) is a tall, evergreen shrub or small tree in the warmest parts of the British Isles and although it grows slowly, it will in time reach 20 feet or more. There are good, flowering specimens to be seen on walls at Kew and in various private gardens near London. Some are shrub-like, about 4 feet tall and carry small yellow flowers 1 inch long in short racemes, during April and May. Their fern-like foliage is as attractive as that of the preceding species. *S. macrocarpa,* native to Chile, was introduced in 1822.

A species quite hardy, with pea-shaped flowers, is *S. viciifolia* (Vicia-leaved: Vetch). It is a deciduous, moderate-sized shrub which many nurserymen recommend should always be grown against a sunny wall, despite the plant's hardiness. It flowers much more freely there and spreads out its young shoots which are usually spiny and show off the delicate, fern-like foliage and blue-white flowers to best advantage. The flowers of the Sophora, like those of many other plants, always come to perfection on a wall.

This particular species, a native of Yunnan, Szechwan and Hupeh, China, where it has been found at altitudes up to 13,500 feet, was introduced to Kew Botanic Gardens in 1897.

Stauntonia hexaphylla (five-leaved) is an evergreen twiner, with long-stalked leaves composed of from 3 to 7 leaflets, leathery in texture, surrounding the stalk. It carries fragrant, unisexual flowers, 3 to 7 in racemes and they are charming in their white and violet colouring. On a wall it makes a thick tangle and will bear fruits in favourable parts of the British Isles. They are purplish, sweet and about the size of a walnut. But unfortunately the plant seldom fruits or even flowers in gardens near London. It can be grown in a cool greenhouse and is then very decorative quite late in the year. Several catalogues describe it under the name *Holboellia hexaphylla* (it is closely related to that genus). The species is a native of Japan and Korea and frequently seen in gardens in China, where some old specimens have stems 6 inches in diameter at the base. It does well in ordinary garden loam. Both Marchant and Hillier have the plant.

Trachelospermum. Two or three species of this genus are offered by nurseries. They are evergreen climbers with clusters of small white or yellowish-white flowers which are delightfully fragrant. The best place for these plants is on the wall of a house or on a wall near a pathway, where the scent of the flowers can be enjoyed. In cold districts *T. jasminoides* is grown in a cool greenhouse, where the scent is always stronger. The plant is less hardy, perhaps, than *T. asiaticum.* This species will go up to a height of 15 feet or more on a wall and may be found in gardens north of London where it is prized for its show of fragrant flowers in late summer.

The growth is dense, the branching stems being coated with hairs. Its leathery, dark glossy green leaves are small, the largest being 2 inches long by ¾ inch wide, oval in shape and cheerful to see all through the winter months. The small, tubular-shaped flowers are yellowish-white, very fragrant, and come in clusters about 2 inches long.

A good specimen may be seen at Kew Botanic Gardens, where it has been growing luxuriantly for many years. The species is a native of Japan and Korea: a charming, hardy, evergreen climber that deserves to be more widely planted in our gardens. The plant often appears under the name of *T. divaricatum.*

T. jasminoides is less hardy and may be distinguished from the other species by its larger leaves and flowers. It is known as the Chinese Jasmine and is a favourite greenhouse twining plant. Outside it is successful only on walls in the south and south-west, where it will carry an abundance of sweet-scented pure white flowers in July and August.

Its leaves are often 3 inches long and 1 inch wide, and the white flowers, which have 5 spreading lobes, measure about 1 inch across. When carried freely they are very charming against the dark glossy green foliage. This species, a native of China, was introduced by Robert Fortune from Shanghai in 1844. On a warm wall in Cornwall it will go up to a height of 10 feet or more.

There are two varieties, viz. var. *japonica*, which has proved hardier and has larger leaves, these turning colour in the autumn and retaining their brilliant shades all through the winter. In the variety *variegatum*, the leaves, which are shorter and broader, are silver-variegated and beautifully coloured bronzy-red and white during the autumn.

Many shrub specialists also offer *S. japonica forma Wilsonii*, a variety introduced from China by Wilson. Its leaves colour well, the plant making a fine foliage-climber for a cool greenhouse.

The *Trachelospermum* like a light, loamy soil and benefit in their young state from an annual mulching of sifted peat.

Propagation is usually by cuttings, which should be taken in August.

Tripterygium is a genus of two climbing, deciduous shrubs, which in this country do best against warm walls. (The generic name is from *tri*, three; and *pteron*, wing; it refers to the three-winged fruits.) They are rare in our gardens. Hillier lists *T. forrestii* (now referred to by most botanists as *T. wilfordii*) and *T. regelii* and states that the first species resembles *Celastrus orbiculatus* in foliage and manner of growth. I have only come across the plant in greenhouses in this country.

T. regelii seems to be hardy and makes a fine rambling wall-shrub up to 20 feet. It grows slowly in most inland gardens. Its foliage, according to Bean, resembles that of the Celastrus; it is a refreshing dark green and attractive all through the summer. The small yellow-white flowers, fragrant, come in terminal panicles about 9 inches long and are at their best in July and August. The fruits, three-angled, each angle with a wing, are greenish-white in colour. Dr. Rehder describes it in *The Standard Cyclopedia of Horticulture*, "A handsome shrub conspicuous chiefly on account of the large bright green foliage contrasting well with the reddish-brown stems. . . . It apparently grows well in any soil." The species is native to Japan, Korea and Formosa.

T. wilfordii, a deciduous climber up to 30 or 40 feet tall, is tender and succeeds only in the south. Good flowering and fruiting specimens can be found in Cornwall and the Isle of Wight. Its chief beauty is its purple-crimson fruits which are 3-winged and hang in long clusters among the green leaves during the autumn months. The leaves are ovalish, from 2 to 6 inches long, toothed, and they are usually glaucous beneath. The flowers, carried in long panicles, are greenish-white and not striking. It is essentially an ornamental fruiting-climber for the autumn; best in a cool greenhouse or on a wall in a warm, sheltered garden. The late Lionel Rothschild had a very fine plant growing in a cool greenhouse at Exbury, Southampton.

T. wilfordii, a native of Yunnan, China, was discovered by Forrest in 1906.

Veronica hulkeana is called the most beautiful of all the shrub species that we grow in the British Isles. It is unfortunately, like so many desirable shrubs, tender and must be grown as a wall-shrub or housed in a cool greenhouse. It is certainly worth a pot or a tub in a sunny part of a greenhouse, and grown in this way will keep to a useful bushy plant 3 or 4 feet high. But it makes such a delightful picture in full bloom out of doors that it should be given a trial whenever possible against a warm wall in sheltered gardens. It will then go up to a height of 6 or 8 feet and, spreading out more openly, better display its glorious panicles of soft lavender flowers. These may be as much as 18 inches long and half as wide. The smallest are probably no less than 6 inches by about 3 inches. The thick, evergreen leaves come in pairs fairly widely spaced on the stems, and are a shining green and coarsely toothed, the largest being 2 inches long and 1 inch wide – broadly oval in shape. I do not know of a Veronica that blooms so profusely as this species. In fact, over-flowering has been thought to cause the shrub to deteriorate after some years. Unfortunately it sometimes dies back completely when it has bloomed profusely through one or two seasons. The individual flowers measure about $\frac{1}{4}$ inch across and are a delicate shade of lavender or lilac – an exquisite colour.

As soon as the flowers fade, they should be removed to prevent the plant from forming seed, which will help to conserve its energy and strengthen it. This lovely wall-shrub usually blooms during May and June and when grown close to a wall should have its tallest branches supported by wires or by trellis, and it will thrive in a light, sandy loam. It is best propagated by 6-inch cuttings of young wood taken in late summer; insert them in sand under glass with a gentle bottom heat. A native of South Island, New Zealand, it was introduced in 1860.

Viburnum fragrans is a completely hardy shrub, one of the best known of the genus, but for the sake of its richly fragrant winter flowers it is often grown against a wall. These begin blooming in November on a wall and go on perhaps to the New Year, and they are safer from frost there than in the open. Furthermore, the shrub planted in the open garden does not begin flowering sometimes till February, and seldom do its flowers come through a severe frost unscathed. On a wall, as at Kew, it goes up to a height of 12 feet or more and spreads out wider; in November the leafless, dark brown branches are thickly covered with small heads of pinkish-white flowers. The plant is a native of Kansu, China, and does best in a good, deep, loamy soil.

Our last family of climbing plants is the Vine (*Vitis*).[1] It is one of the largest and is probably the oldest: the common Grape Vine, *V. vinifera*, goes far back in the history of horticulture; this plant (also decorative when its foliage colours in the autumn) and the common Hop were among the first climbers grown by man. A variety of the common Grape, *V. vinifera purpurea*, is widely planted as an ornamental foliage-climber in our gardens today. (A specimen exhibited by the Sunningdale Nurseries, Windlesham, Surrey, in October, 1958, at the R.H.S. Show, received an Award of Merit. The plant has purple, 3- to 5-lobed leaves about 6 inches across and bears bunches of small purplish grapes in the autumn.)

We don't know the native habitat of the Grape Vine, *V. vinifera*. It is thought to come from different parts of Asia Minor. Humboldt, the German naturalist (1769–1859) says, "The Vine does not belong to Europe; it grows wild on the coasts of the Caspian Sea, in Armenia and in Caramanica. From Asia it

[1] An old Latin name for the vine.

passed into Greece, and thence into Sicily. The Phocaeans carried it into the South of France; the Romans planted it on the Banks of the Rhine. The species of *Vitis* which are found wild in North America, and which gave the name of the land of the Vine (Winenland) to the first part of the new continent which was discovered by Europeans, are very different from our *Vitis vinifera*."

V. aestivalis is one of the native American Vines. It is known as the Summer Grape and from it are descended some good fruiting varieties such as 'Cynthiana' and 'Virginia Seedling'. It grows wild in the eastern and central United States and bears small, palatable black fruits in the autumn. Its leaves colour well but it is not such a fine ornamental climber as its near relative, *V. bicolor* (two-coloured).

This species (the Blue Grape) is a strong tendril climber with leaves from 4 to 12 inches long and as wide, 3- or 5-lobed, which are strikingly coloured with a bluish bloom underneath; above they are a dull green. The two colours show up well in the sun, and then the leaves are most beautiful when they hang down from a pergola or the top of an arbour. It is magnificent on a tree, along with the scarlet-berrying *Celastrus scandens*.

V. coignetiae (named for Mme Coignet of Lyons, who introduced seed of the species from Japan in 1875). Hillier's catalogue describes it as "The grandest of all ornamental Vines". It is one of the most vigorous, climbing up to a height of 60 or 90 feet on trees in its habitat, Japan. Its leaves are probably the largest in the genus, often measuring 12 inches long and as much across. A gardener once grew it on a sunny wall (having heard it called the Crimson Glory Vine) and left it to climb by its own efforts. But this it cannot do, as it climbs by means of its long-branched tendrils, which twine round twigs and stems but have no adhesive discs as do members of the *Parthenocissus* Section (now described by most botanists as a separate genus). Trellis had to be rigged up for the plant. It would have climbed up stout stakes, however: half a dozen or so, with branching side pieces, rammed down into the soil. It soon reaches the top of a wall and trails down the other side.[1]

[1] A magnificent specimen grows on a south wall at the University Botanic Gardens, Oxford. At the end of April the young, undeveloped leaves, 4 inches across, are a bright yellowish-green; and the tiny flower-clusters emerald-green.

The leaves, broadly heart-shaped, with 3 or 5 lobe-like points, turn a brilliant crimson in the autumn and are gloriously decorative when the sun shines through them. The grapes are ½ inch wide, very unpalatable, although apparently when they are frozen they are eaten and relished by the Japanese.

V. davidii. Two kinds are offered by nurseries, viz. the type plant and *V. davidii cyanocarpa* (blue-fruited). The species, a native of China, was introduced by Wilson in 1900, but was probably here in cultivation under the name of *V. spinovitis davidii* about 1885. One of its attractions is its young shoots and leaf-stalks clothed with hooked bristles. The heart-shaped leaves, toothed, measure from 4 to 10 inches long and 2 to 8 inches wide; they are a shining dark green above and bluish-green beneath. In the autumn they turn a brilliant red. It is a tall-growing Vine, very beautiful on a Larch tree, where I have seen it growing in some gardens, in company with the variety *cyanocarpa*, which has larger leaves; these become more brilliantly coloured than those of the type. Hillier lists it as "a less prickly variety, with bluish fruits". The fruits of both plants are edible and sweet.

V. flexuosa var. *parvifolia* is one of the smallest-leaved of all the Vines. It was introduced from Central China in 1900 and is the most suitable for walls or pergolas. Its leaves, 3- or 5-lobed, are from 2 to 3 inches long, a vivid glossy green above and purplish or bronzy beneath. Trained on a whitewashed wall, it is most effective, and it also makes a rich green background for low-growing flowering shrubs.

V. henryana is one of the *Parthenocissus* Group (*P. henryana*) and clings to flat surfaces by its disc-tipped tendrils, which mostly have 5 or 7 slender branches. It is thus ideal for a wall, and there it does better than anywhere else, except on a shady wall in a cool greenhouse (where it must be grown in cold districts). A delightful foliage-climber, which unfortunately is sometimes a failure in inland gardens, although if it is grown on a sheltered wall facing north it should survive the winter weather. L. H. Bailey describes the plant as being tender in America, "The colouring of the leaves is more beautiful when it is grown in the greenhouse or outdoors in a partly shaded place, in full sun the leaves lose finally the white markings and the purple colour."

The leaves are composed of 3 to 5 leaflets, 1½ to 5 inches long and tapered to both ends. Their beauty is in the dark velvety-green colour and the silver-white and pink variegation of the veins; the undersides are purplish. In late autumn the leaves turn a bright red. The fruits are dark blue. Marchant lists the plant as *Parthenocissus henryana*. A native of Central China, it was discovered by Henry in 1885 and introduced by Wilson for Veitch's nursery in 1900.

V. heterophylla belongs to the *Ampelopsis* Section and is often given that generic name. It supports its long, luxuriant stems by twining tendrils and is a magnificent autumnal-tinting climber for a wall. It will climb trellis or branched stakes set in a row. Its leaves are very variable, sometimes heart-shaped and entire, sometimes lobed, on the same plant; they measure from 2 to 4 inches in length. The small berries are a pretty shade of porcelain blue, dotted with black, and when freely borne very decorative in the autumn. To get a good crop, the plant must be grown in full sun on a south wall. There is a charming variety called *elegans*, which has pinkish young shoots and leaves touched with pink and white. A delicate-looking Vine which is often grown in a hanging basket and will succeed outdoors only on a warm wall.

The species, a native of China, Japan and Korea, was introduced in 1860.

V. himalayana. A vigorous Vine of the *Parthenocissus* Group (*P. himalayana*) from the Himalayas, where it is found growing at altitudes up to 11,000 feet. It is not, however, particularly hardy in our gardens and needs a warm wall. A beautiful foliage-climber, where it can be grown; and one which clings to walls and flat surfaces with its adhesive-tipped tendrils. The leaves are composed of 3 leaflets, 2 to 5 inches long, dark green above, paler and glaucous beneath; they turn a rich, glowing red in the autumn.

The variety *rubrifolia* (introduced from West China in 1907) has smaller leaves which are a pretty purplish colour in the spring.

Hillier has both plants. The catalogue describes the species, "A self-clinging Himalayan *Ampelopsis* differing from the Virginia Creeper in its larger leaflets." Some botanists have placed it in the *Ampelopsis* Group.

V. inconstans (or *P. tricuspidata*) is described by many nurseries as the most popular self-clinging wall climber. It clings to brickwork (like the preceding plant) with disc-tipped tendrils and is one of the best autumn-tinting plants grown in our gardens. The leaves are very variable. On young plants they are small; on adult plants they are often from 8 to 10 inches wide, the largest coming on the lower stems. The smallest, ovalish or 3-foliolate, measure from 2 to 5 inches across.

The yellowish-green flowers, insignificant, as are most of the Vine flowers, come in small clusters, and the small fruits which follow turn an attractive dark blue in the autumn. Dr. Rehder quotes the popular names, Japanese Ivy and Boston Ivy, and says it is a hardy plant that makes a dense covering for walls. "The glossy foliage stands dust and smoke well and turns to a brilliant orange and scarlet in fall. Probably the favourite of all hardy Vines in cities."

The species, a native of Japan and China, was introduced by John Gould Veitch in 1862. It can be got from most nurseries and a few years back cost 7s. 6d. per plant.

V. megalophylla (large-leaved). The leaves, composed of many leaflets (often 60) measure 1 to 2 feet in length; the leaflets vary in size and shape, and are a deep green colour above and glaucous beneath. It is a vigorous plant, climbing up to 30 feet tall by means of its twining tendrils, and needing a tall tree to show off the foliage to best advantage. This species will make shoots as much as 10 feet long in a season. The fruits, $\frac{1}{4}$ inch wide, purple first, then black, come in clusters 4 inches across and when freely borne are very decorative in the autumn.

The species, a native of Western China, was introduced to France by Maurice de Vilmorin in 1894 and later by Wilson, who collected it for Messrs. Veitch's nursery in 1900.

V. micans (sparkling). The epithet no doubt refers to the glittering green upper surface of the leaves, which is delightfully conspicuous in full sunlight. They are slightly glaucous underneath, 3-lobed, the divisions not always prominent, and from 2 to 5 inches long. It is a tall-growing Vine, up to 20 feet in height, and may be used with charming effect on pergolas and arbours. There is a fine specimen on the pergola at Kew Botanic Gardens.

The variety, *cinerea* (named by Rehder) has leaves sometimes covered with greyish down on both sides.

Both plants (*Ampelopsis*) have twining tendrils and climb quickly when once established in a good loam. The species is a native of Szechwan and Hupeh.

V. orientalis is another *Ampelopsis* and a choice climber for an upright of a pergola. It mostly makes a loose, bushy Vine and prospers in a position where it gets plenty of sun. On a south wall it fruits well, the berries hanging in glossy, red clusters – they have been likened to large red currants. The leaves are variable; they have 9 leaflets, from 1 to 3 inches long and ½ to 2 inches wide; they are coarsely-toothed, a dull green above and a greyish-green beneath. This Vine grows well on a trellis and is a charming covering for a wall. It is very similar to the North American *V. arborea* (*Ampelopsis arborea*), a Vine with bright green, finely divided leaves.

V. orientalis is a native of Asia Minor, where it flourishes luxuriantly in mountainous regions at altitudes up to 5,000 feet.

V. striata (striate: marked with fine parallel lines or grooves). The species is now mostly described under *Cissus*. It is the only evergreen Vine we grow and rather tender. A graceful climber, with thread-like tendrils, for adorning a wall in a cold greenhouse. The leaves are 5-foliolate, the leaflets, scarcely stalked, measuring from ½ inch to 1½ inches long and about half as wide; they are coarsely-toothed and attractive all through the year. The foliage is luxuriant and beautiful in its finely-cut divisions. The fruits are small, reddish-purple and apparently on some plants a deep red and more striking. In warm maritime districts this rare Vine may be grown outside on a wall; near London and in inland gardens it should be housed. In the wild and in warm climates its stems reach a height of 60 feet or more. Its habitat is Chile and Southern Brazil. A charming Vine for a pot. Many florists sell it as a foliage-plant for indoor decoration.

V. thomsonii received the Royal Horticultural Society's First Class Certificate in 1903. A fine, decorative climber, its leaves purplish at first, then passing through greenish-purple to deep red-purple and crimson in the autumn. Dr. Rehder says it is tender in the U.S.A. It has proved completely hardy in Britain and is among the most beautiful of the self-clinging Vines for walls. I remember seeing it on a high wall on which a Wistaria was trained; the Vine spreading out its young purplish foliage along the lower part of the wall, while the pale lavender racemes of the Wistaria hung above it. A charming association of foliage and flowers. This species has leaves usually composed of 5 leaflets, 1 to 4 inches long and about half as wide. It was introduced from China in 1900.

V. vinifera (vine-bearing) is the common Grape Vine. It has produced palatable grapes in our sunny districts and good wine has been made from the fruit. The varieties such as *apiifolia*, the Cut-leaved or Parsley Vine; and var. *purpurea* (already described) are good ornamental climbers for trellis-work on walls or for trees or pergolas.

The Parsley Vine has leaves with 3 or 5 divisions and these are again divided into narrow lobes. Its elegant foliage shows up to advantage on a white stone object – a white-washed wall or the upright of a pergola is ideal. The plant climbs by its tendrils, which twine readily round supporting wires.

Var. *purpurea* is magnificent on a tree when the sun catches the purple-reddish leaves and lights up their colour. Marchant offers var. 'Brant', "A free-growing, hardy, fruiting Vine. The foliage changes in autumn through yellow and orange to rosy-crimson and scarlet." It was priced some years back at 6s. 6d. per plant.

V. vitacea is often called the Common Virginia Creeper, but it is not the true plant and is distinguished from it chiefly by its tendrils, which have no adhesive discs and therefore cannot cling to flat surfaces. It climbs by twining its tendrils round twigs and stems and will scramble over bushes and trail down over walls or fences. The leaf-structure is the same as in the true Virginia Creeper: the 5 leaflets radiate from a long, common stalk, but they are larger and of a brighter shade of green. This species is thought to be native to North-east America; it has been grown in our gardens since 1824. Most gardeners prefer it to the self-clinging species, for it is the more gorgeously coloured of the two. All these Vines prosper in loamy soils and are easily increased by layering. If we grow *V. heterophylla*, however, we must remember to give it a restricted root-run, for it will then fruit much more freely.

CHAPTER FOUR

Pergolas

[1]

Vines are usually associated with pergolas. They were important features in the gardens of the ancient Egyptians and the peoples of the Mediterranean regions, who built them primarily to provide shady walks, and chose mostly the Vine to cover them. Set close together, the plants soon made an overhead mass of foliage dense enough to ward off the hot sun; and another reason, equally important, for planting the Vine was for the grapes it bore.

The earliest pergolas were often constructed of wooden props. Another pergola-like feature common in the gardens of these ancient peoples was the trellis-work covered with Vines which surrounded a well, "inviting the owner and his family to gather beneath its shade" – a sort of circular pergola. (The word is from the Latin *pergula*, a projecting roof, shed, or Vine arbour.)

Later, in the Italian gardens of the Renaissance, pergolas were magnificent structures of marble with hard-wood horizontals, across which the Vines grew, the bunches of fruit hanging down along the whole length of the walk.

Even in our country, where 'shady walks' are not greatly in demand, crude wooden structures for Vines were erected long before the introduction of the pergola. William Horman, in his *Vulgaris*, published in 1519, mentioned, "Alleys in gardens covered with Vines railed up with stakes to provide shadow in the parching heat . . . the Vine clinging to his rails with his twining strings and let hang down his clusters of grapes."

Although the pergola belongs to the warm, sunny South, and is there a valuable garden feature, it is not without its uses in our cooler climate. Certainly it doesn't need roofing-in or over with dense foliage; and no doubt pergolas are more useful in our southern gardens where they can be built in open sunny places. Furthermore, they need ample space, the more elaborate structures of stone and brick being suitable only for large pleasure-grounds. There are many fine examples of contemporary work to be seen in different parts of the country. At Encombe, Sandgate, Mr. Basil Ionides has designed a pergola of white-washed stone columns with white marble capitals and cross-pieces of white wood. It supports a few Vines: the effect of the green leaves against the white stone-work is startling in its simplicity.

To give variety to the structures, both round and square pillars are sometimes used as in the pergola in the Deanery Garden at Sonning. The roofing horizontals to carry the plants are of oak. (It may be a matter of personal preference, but red brick and tiles seem more in keeping with the English garden scene than marble or white stone-work.) Another fine example is in the garden at Marshcourt; the pergola, designed by Sir Edwin Lutyens, has its piers or columns built of red tiles, and the horizontals are of dark oak. A magnificent piece of work, which has an ideal setting.

For small gardens wooden structures are usually best. Many amateurs build their own pergolas, using brick or stone. And I have known some enterprising people make their stone columns from cement. It was done quite cheaply with one part cement and three parts sand, mixed to a fairly thick consistency and poured into cylindrical moulds of strong cardboard prepared in sections. Iron or steel rods, bought for next to nothing from a scrap-iron dealer's, were inserted in the middle of the cement to reinforce it – in one case old brass stair-rods firmly wired together were used. The piers or columns when finally completed were 8 feet high, each measuring about 9 inches across the base – slender columns suitable for a small pergola. These were then painted over with one of the proprietary white cement mixtures and looked like good quality stone.

Bricks and tiles are dearer. It is possible sometimes to get old bricks from a demolition site, many good enough to build with. The old-fashioned 2-inch red bricks are best, of course, but expensive. Wooden uprights, by far the cheapest material and the most easily erected, are used by many gardeners today.

Before the choice of material, however, comes the question of site. The important thing to remember is that a pergola is a covered walk which must lead somewhere. In a small, modern garden where often there is only a single narrow path, it wouldn't be advisable to cover it with a pergola. On the other hand it is possible to lay down a path, beginning near the house and leading to a seat at the other side of the garden, and to cover part of the walk with a pergola.

The site should get plenty of sun; it should in fact be the sunniest spot in the garden. Next, the length and width of the structure must be decided upon. This will naturally depend on the size of the garden and the space available. The pathway or walk must be wide enough to enable two people to walk side by side in comfort. I suggest 4 feet as the minimum. But I have seen pergola-walks less than that in width; and one so narrow that people had to walk in single file along it.

As regards height, the columns or piers should average about 8 feet—not much less. I have recollections of walking through one pergola, in which the columns were about 7 feet high. Every so often it was necessary to stoop to dodge the ornamental Gourds which hung from the stems trained over the wooden cross-pieces. Some garden-designers maintain, however, that the walk should be as wide as the columns are high. Such a capacious structure could of course be erected only in a very large garden.

The material for building, whether stone or brick or wood, must harmonize with the house. Hardwoods are all right; they look well with practically any type of house (oak and teak are the most permanent). For small pergolas wood is very suitable. Heavy white stone, or marble, is quite out of place in a small garden surrounding a small house. These luxury materials must be left to the owners of mansions and large pleasure-grounds.

Home-made cement columns (referred to at the beginning of the chapter) are favoured by many gardeners; these columns have the virtue of being permanent and, if not massive and heavy-looking, are suitable for a smallish pergola. They must have a good, solid foundation and should be set about 6 feet apart. The wooden horizontals, often of oak, may be fixed in grooves made in the tops of the columns.

Wood is mostly used for the cross-beams. When these are used for bracing wooden uprights, they carry the horizontals running longwise; the cross-beams should have a slight upward curve, the camber giving added strength to the wood. Cross-beams and horizontals must be firmly jointed together. On flimsier structures made, say, of wooden poles, they may be bound together with felt-covered wire. Chains covered with rope or thick cord are sometimes used as horiontals, but they lack the grace and solidity of the wood. The rope or cord is necessary to protect the climbers from the intense cold of the bare iron in winter.

Wooden structures are the easiest and quickest to build and can be erected single-handed. The ends of the uprights which are to be sunk in the ground are first charred up to, or just above, the ground-line to prevent them from rotting. Or the ends may be treated with some kind of wood-preservative. The roofing beams may either be nailed to one another or jointed together. The latter method is the better.

It is unwise to attempt to build anything elaborate. Those who can afford it will, of course, employ an experienced landscape gardener to design the pergola and carry out the work.

As regards choice of plants, the type of pergola will decide this: some climbers are totally unsuited for training up columns and many would be quite out of place on a small pergola.

One immediately thinks of the Vines as the most suitable; and some of the self-clinging species with their finely-divided leaves are ideal. The large-leaved, coarser varieties can be used only on big, stone columns; and probably one will be enough. Wistaria, too, looks best on heavy stonework. In time it makes a thick woody trunk which would look out of place against a slender wooden upright.

Clematis are lovely on any type of pergola but need supporting, unless the long horizontals happen to be chains.

Climbing Roses, too, need tying round the columns but will usually clamber without any assistance over the cross-pieces.

The mistake of overplanting must be avoided. The architectural detail must never be obscured by a superfluity of flowers, foliage and creeping stems.

If it is thought that the bare lower stem of a climber is something of an eyesore, a dwarf shrub may be planted against it at the foot of the column. For my part, I consider any bare stem attractive twined round a white stone column. On wood or on weathered stone it is scarcely noticeable.

Walls and Buildings

[2]

VINES are grown not only on pergolas but on walls. In ancient times the vine-dressers of Persia trained their Vines to run up a wall and curl over on the top.

There are several species which will cling to brickwork by means of their tendrils which have sucker-like pads at the tips. But in this country we seldom use walls for Vines; in warm, southern gardens the fruiting varieties do reasonably well it is true, though the grapes are not always palatable. We prefer something more showy, a climber, for instance, that needs plenty of sun and warmth to bring its flowers to perfection.

On the other hand, there are some, like the Flame-flower (*Tropaeolum speciosum*), which need a north wall and a moist root-run. The soil at the base is cool and seldom dries out.

As regards the walls of a house, we have a choice of three or four. (Fortunate owners of walled gardens have twice as many.) Where there is a boundary-wall which can be viewed from the house, it should be used, I think, for some of the winter climbers such as *Clematis calycina* and *C. cirrhosa*, both slightly tender. A wall facing due north is best, for the frosted plants then have a chance to thaw out slowly before the sun reaches them and discolours the flowers. Such a wall is best, too, for the Winter Jasmine; its bright yellow flowers always last longer against a protective background of brick. As this straggling climber responds well to pruning, it may be grown against the low wall under a living-room window. Odd, untidy flowering shoots spring up, which can be seen from indoors. Winter Sweet (*Chimonanthus praecox*) should also be grown on the house because the flowers are so richly fragrant. They are not much to look at, in fact they are so insignificant and colourless that they are not easily discerned from a distance on grey winter days. It is their scent which is important. This climber should be grown on every house.

Unfortunately there is not much space on the front wall of most small houses; but there is at least height; we can therefore train the plants upward and get a good show of flowers or berries that way. The side walls, often with only one upper window, are more suitable and, indeed, are sometimes completely covered with different types of climbers; but a single one is far more arresting than three or four crowded together.

Although the association of common Ivy and the Climbing Rose 'Albertine' sounds odd, it is lovely and quite suitable for a smallish space; the dark green Ivy leaves contrast strikingly with the pinkish-apricot flowers. The rose needs trellis or wires to support it, but the Ivy, with its stem-roots, will climb unaided up any brickwork.

Is a wall damaged by having creepers growing on it? Some people think so. Thick, evergreen foliage on single brick walls often causes dampness to infiltrate through to the inside plaster. Virginia Creeper and others which shed their leaves do not appear to do any damage, however.

On brick walls the aerial roots of Ivy have been known to do much damage to the pointing, eating their way into the cement and causing it to deteriorate. When the main stem has been severed at the base to kill the plant, the upper, spreading growths must not be pulled off, otherwise the cement will come away with the roots which have grown into it. Ivy must always be allowed to die off naturally.

Deciduous climbers are best for single-brick walls; it is perhaps wiser, however, to leave them bare. Some builders advocate painting them with damp-resisting paint and leaving it to weather for a year before anything is planted.

Ivy and Virginia Creeper, if kept well under control, add greatly to the charm of a building. Grown up the base to a height of about 4 feet, these climbers give richness to the brick- or stone-work, or they will emphasize the beauty of some architectural details, the Ivy, for example, following the flowing lines of a Romanesque arch. At Compton Wynyates in Warwick- shire, Ivy is grown round some of the lattice windows and regu- larly pruned to prevent it from spreading too far.

It must never be allowed to grow unattended and unchecked and to cover up any architectural detail. Overgrowth has ruined the appearance of many valuable old buildings. The late seven- teenth-century gateway at Groombridge Place in Kent had Ivy planted against one of its piers many years ago, which soon covered the fine stone-work.

A surprising number of historic buildings in this country are smirched with Ivy. For many years the cloisters at Magdalen, Oxford, were covered with it and the beauty of the ancient stone-work was consequently lost to us. It grows so thick on the walls of some cottages in the south of England that no brick-work is visible; and unwisely the creeping stems have been allowed to reach the eaves and get into the guttering. Ivy is insidious stuff and needs watching.

It is sometimes pointed out that a wall of a house planted with climbers provides a connecting link between the building and the garden. In one property this relationship was manifested by the west wall covered with a climbing scarlet rose and the same rose in bush form planted in a wide bed beneath it, the bed extending as far as the pathway.

Although Vines are less often grown on walls than Ivy, they are favourite climbers for covering arbours. In hot countries they are trained to form natural arbours, the stems rising up and in the course of years becoming thick and strong enough to support themselves.

In this country trees and tall shrubs of weeping habit are used; these make the best natural arbours. Laburnum, with its supple branches, is a special favourite and when it carries its long hanging racemes of yellow flowers is remarkably beautiful. Some sort of frame-work of strong wood or wire is required, which can be removed when the tree has attained the necessary shape. Wistaria is often trained over a Laburnum arbour, the fragrant mauve flowers and the yellow making a charming picture.

An arbour made of wood is easily and quickly erected. Criss-cross, narrow slats (or ordinary trellis) are used. It is a rather flimsy structure and not very permanent – ideal, however, for slender, soft-stemmed annual climbers. Arbours are less popular nowadays; no doubt they have been superseded by the comfortable modern garden furniture including the shady, portable swing-seat.

Treillage (ornamental lattice-work usually of metal) belongs also to the past; the name is probably unknown to many gardeners of today. In the nineteenth century treillage was used as a supporting tunnel-like archway for Vines, the plants being trained over it, a feature comparable to the pleached alley of the seventeenth century. This was a double row of trees (mostly fruit-trees) planted opposite one another, their branches being trained to form a pleasant shady archway.

Pleached alleys, treillage and arbours may be seen in the grounds of many of our old historic houses where too there is usually a pergola designed by some eminent landscape-gardener of the past. Gardeners are still building pergolas and rightly, for they are not only decorative features in themselves but display the flowers and foliage of climbers better than most things.

CHAPTER FIVE

Climbers and Wall Shrubs
in Plant Associations

❧

Pʟᴀɴᴛ association is a fascinating branch of gardening. The formal flower-beds of the Victorians are a good example, though the garish effect of scarlet geraniums and bright blue lobelia is disliked by some of us, furthermore we find that the planting-out takes up too much time. Perhaps this work is best left to the professional gardeners: the big beds, with their intricate 'ribbon' planting and patterns, which they design so skilfully, are a feature of our parks and public gardens.

Flowers, annual and perennial, may be associated with shrubs, and shrubs with trees, and climbers used with all of them. And these plant associations (leaving out the annuals) are permanent. Which is what most of us busy gardeners want nowadays.

The important thing of course is to choose flowering-plants that bloom at the same time and they should thrive in the same kind of soil. The chief difficulty here, though, is if one happens to dislike lime and the other needs it – providing the right texture for them is not so difficult. (See page 194.)

The association of *Cotoneaster horizontalis* and *Jasminum nudiflorum* was mentioned in Chapter 3. Both flourish in any ordinary garden loam and do well against a west wall. They should be set fairly close together so that the yellow flowers of the one mingle with the bright red berries of the other. The flowers come first, usually they open in November; and the berries will be red a few weeks later. When both plants have grown big, the long stems of the Jasmine can be threaded through the thick, spreading branches of the Cotoneaster – only one side of the Jasmine will then need supporting by wires or by nailing to the brickwork.

In some warm, sheltered gardens the yellow Jasmine is trained on a wall facing north and in front of it, *Camellia sasanqua*, with single, open, rose-pink flowers, is planted. This is one of the loveliest associations for the winter months. A more striking effect is obtained when three or four Jasmines are used, placed about 4 feet apart, against the wall, and several Camellias are grouped together in front. The yellow flowers will be massed thickly together on the wall and there will be a richer show of pink Camellias. The shrubs need a lime-free, leafy soil and the Jasmine does best in ordinary loam; if the soil is thought to be too acid for it, coarse sand and ashes should be dug in before planting.

A great deal can be done with this winter Jasmine. Grow it as a low hedge under window and mass pink-flowered winter heathers in front. Varieties such as *Erica carnea* 'Springwood Pink' with bright rose flowers and any of the Backhouse Hybrids are ideal for the purpose. They don't mind a little lime – though they do best in peaty, acid soils.

It will be necessary to prune the Jasmine every March, when its flowering season is over, to keep it low and bushy. The plant responds well to an annual cutting and will flower profusely every winter.

In an open woodland it can be planted among the dwarf evergreen shrub *Mahonia* (*Berberis*) *aquifolium*, with holly-shaped leaves, which turn bronzy-red in November. The yellow star-shaped Jasmine flowers on the long, arching stems show up beautifully against the red, polished foliage of the shrubs. The Jasmine must not be pruned: its stems must be allowed to ramble freely.

On a wall, where undoubtedly it is always at its best, it can also be used as a background to some of the winter-blooming Rhododendrons: *R. mucronulatum*, for example, a deciduous species with small lavender-rose, bell-shaped flowers, which are often at their loveliest in January. Another companion for it is the dwarf evergreen hybrid, *R.* × *praecox*, with small, glossy green leaves and rose-purple open bells. Plant as groundwork to the shrubs some of the deeper pink Ericas mentioned above.

During the winter months colour in the garden is doubly welcome, and for a show of cheerful yellow nothing can beat this tough, climbing Jasmine. It is often planted in conjunction with *Viburnum fragrans*, which blooms at the same time and has small white flowers (pinkish-white in the bud), which are more fragrant than those of any other winter flower I know. They come thickly on the leafless branches, when the shrub is trained against a wall; and as the branches go up to a height of 12 feet or more in such a position and spread out as wide, plenty of room must be left between the two plants – at least 8 feet. Both like the same sort of soil: a fairly loose garden loam.

Where the Vines (*Vitis*) are grown, some magnificent effects of coloured foliage are to be had during the autumn; and the beauty of the leaves will be enhanced by the scarlet and orange fruits of other climbers. Bean mentions *Vitis bicolor* growing in a tangle with *Celastrus scandens* in the wild.

Both are amenable to woodland culture in this country. The leaves of the Vine are bluish-white underneath and colour well in October; and the Celastrus will be in fruit (vivid scarlet-orange) at the same time. They should be planted on the edge of the woodland with some dark green conifers in the background to show up the colours.

Celastrus orbiculatus is more often seen in our gardens and it gives a remarkable display of fruit. Many gardeners find that it is a more reliable berrying plant than the other species. Its fruits are as vividly coloured as those of *C. scandens*.

I have seen *Vitis bicolor* and *Celastrus orbiculatus* trained over the November Cherry (*Prunus subhirtella autumnalis*), which in its bush form has wide-spreading branches, strong enough to carry the weight of the climbers. And the tangle of their stems did not prevent the shrub from blooming freely after the berries and the leaves of the climbers had fallen.

Another striking association for the autumn garden is *Vitis henryana* grown in conjunction with the brilliant autumn-tinting *Berberis thunbergii*. This Berberis is perhaps the most brilliantly-coloured of all autumn-tinting shrubs; its small leaves turn vivid shades of orange, scarlet and crimson in late October. Several specimens should be set in front of the Vine, which is best grown on a north wall; it is a self-clinging species and adheres to flat surfaces by means of its disc-tipped tendrils. The dark green leaves, which are variegated with silvery-white and pink, turn deep red in autumn and make a warm, glowing background to the brilliant colours of the shrubs. The best place for this Vine is a north wall, where it is well sheltered. It seldom thrives on trees in the open garden.

The large-leaved Vine, *Vitis coignetiae* (leaves sometimes 12 inches long and as wide), turns a glowing scarlet in autumn, and grown on a tall, white-stemmed Birch, is a picture on its own. But those who want a companion for it should plant *Clematis tangutica* in the foreground: support it with stakes or let it ramble over the ground. This is the yellow-flowered Clematis, which blooms late; and it has a second season when it carries masses of large, silky, silvery-white seed-heads. The Vine will need tying till it reaches the branches of the Birch. A magnificent display of silver seeds and scarlet foliage.

Both climbers like a good, rich loam to start off in, and it will be necessary to remove all fibrous tree-roots from the ground before the climbers are planted. The Vine will need no further feeding, for, like most autumn-colouring plants, it seems to give the finest display of tints in impoverished soils.

V. coignetiae is sometimes used on a wall, trained on trellis on one side and allowed to trail down the other, the scarlet leaves looking particularly handsome against grey stone-work. And next to it the twining *Actinidia kolomikta* may be planted, giving the climbers plenty of room in which to develop. This makes a striking association: white and pink leaves of the Actinidia (delicate-looking) contrasting with the glowing, heavy, scarlet leaves of the Vine.

Try this Actinidia, with its beautifully variegated foliage, in association with the Berberis just described. The shrub will reach a height of about 6 feet and make a good support for the twiner, whose whitish-pink leaves will show up well against the tiny leaves of the Berberis as they begin to change from bright green to yellow and orange.

A climber not often seen in our gardens is *Aconitum volubile* (twining), a plant with long, slender stems which die down

187

during the winter months. Its small helmet-shaped flowers, a violet-blue, come in rather loose, drooping racemes and bloom from August to October. Nothing could be more suitable for growing on *Berberis thunbergii*: its leaves will be yellow and its berries scarlet when the blue flowers are at their best. Two or three shrubs should be planted together and the Aconitum allowed to run freely over them.

Spring gives us a great variety of climbers and consequently a wider range of plant associations, many of which are successful in the open garden. My first choice, however, is a wall shrub: *Forsythia suspensa* with golden-yellow bell-flowers. Plant in front of it the Grape Hyacinths (*Muscari* 'Heavenly Blue') or the deeper sky-blue *Chionodoxa sardensis* ('Glory of the Snow'), a tiny Scilla-like flower. It is necessary, of course, to have plenty of them to make a spreading mass of deep blue at the foot of the yellow *Forsythia*. A glorious combination of colours.

On a north wall, where this shrub is often grown and where it will always give a profusion of yellow blossom, it may be associated with some of the flowering Quince (*Chaenomeles lagenaria*): the type plant has vivid red flowers, which are, I think, a little startling against the bright yellow. The apple blossom-pink of var. 'Moesloesii' is a softer colour and blends well with yellow; it will perhaps be preferred by most people. Leave plenty of room between these shrubs, for they are wide-spreading. The ends of the branches will soon touch, which enables the flowers to mingle, but they should not be bunched up too closely.

One of the first spring-blooming Clematis is the species *C. alpina*, with blue-purplish flowers 3 inches wide: a dwarf climber, about 6 feet tall, and well adapted to a low wall. It is often planted on the north side and trained to trail down the other side in the sun. A good plant to go with it is the wall shrub *Kerria japonica* var. *plena*, with double orange-yellow flowers which come at the same time as the blue Clematis flowers. Set the shrub on the south side of the wall in such a position that the blue Clematis flowers are not hidden by its tall branches. The root of the Clematis should be at least 5 feet to the left or the right of the shrub, which will be on the other (the south) side of the wall.

It is possible, of course, to grow the two together in full sun and train the Clematis through the branches of the shrub. As the climber needs shade round its roots, a dwarf evergreen plant like *Mahonia aquifolium* should be planted in front of it. (This ground cover can be kept down to 18 inches by an annual drastic pruning of the plant.)

The Clematis will make its own way up and through the branches of the Kerria, the leaf-tendrils, as soon as they touch a slender branch, curling round like a ring and taking the stem upward to the top of the bush. The blue star-shaped flowers look charming among the orange-yellow ones of the Kerria.

White Clematis need a dark, contrasting background to show off their flowers well; and nothing could be better than a closely-clipped, black-green Yew hedge. The white *Florida* variety called 'Lucie Lemoine' is a magnificent sight trained along some low support in front of a Yew hedge. In a garden in Clonmel, Southern Ireland, this climber is carefully trained on strong bamboo canes which are bent elliptically (each end fixed firmly into the soil) to form a 'wave' effect along the ground. Several rows are used. The stems grow along the curved bamboos, giving an uncommonly beautiful effect of white flower 'waves' against the black Yew. A Clematis trained in this way needs far more attention than it would do if it were grown in a normal way up a wire-trellis against a wall. In this position it needs little pruning. But 'shaping' it over an elaborate support such as that just described entails plenty of work. It will be advisable to have two plants of the same variety, one set at each end of the single row of bamboos. (Four for 2 rows, and so on.) The main stems will then only have to grow half the distance of the bamboo framework. Furthermore, by keeping the main stem shorter (each plant will only have to travel half the length of the framework) the Clematis will bloom more freely, the lower part of the stem being covered with flowers as well as the extreme end.

Clematis montana, the Himalayan species, is not a suitable type for this formal treatment and must be planted where it can grow with the greatest of freedom: on a high tree or over a long veranda or a wall. Similarly, the pink variety *C. montana rubens* should not be restricted. They are not suitable types for drastic 'shaping'.

A beautiful companion for this pink-flowered Clematis, one that can accompany it on a tree or a bush, is the Vine called *Vitis flexuosa parvifolia*, which has small leaves (about 3 inches long) a brilliant green above and purple beneath. The greenish-purple effect of the foliage will be most conspicuous when the pink Clematis flowers are at their best. I have seen these climbers covering an arbour, the pink Clematis growing up one side and the purple-leaved Vine up the other, the two making an exquisite blend of colours on top.

Some of the earliest of the hybrid Clematis begin blooming when *C. montana* and the pink *rubens* are at their best. *C. patens*, which has produced well-known kinds like the purple 'Duke of Edinburgh' and 'Miss Bateman', is a fine species to grow with *C. montana rubens*. They should be planted side by side on a trellis against a west wall; the smaller pink flowers of the *montana* plant harmonize beautifully with the large purple flowers of the species *C. patens* (these are 5 or 6 inches in diameter).

On the front wall of a house *Wistaria* will begin flowering in late May; it is one of the best places for it; I have seen it associated with the *Patens* Clematis called 'Lasurstern', which has large, open, deep blue flowers. This Clematis isn't a tall climber, but its flowers, growing flat against the brickwork, are a charming foil to the lavender hanging racemes of the Wistaria. The darker purple 'Duke of Edinburgh' is even more effective.

Lavender-coloured Wistaria and yellow Laburnum: both flower at the same time, and the shape of their hanging racemes is similar. *Laburnum alpina* has racemes 12 inches long, which open in June; it is perhaps better than the other species, the Common Laburnum, *L. anagyroides*, which has smaller, earlier-blooming flowers – though I have seen them all flowering together in gardens near London.

Although the Wistaria can be trained on the Laburnum, this twiner is usually planted on a wall against which the tree is grown; and when the twining stems are long enough they are trained over into the branches of the Laburnum. No doubt the reason for this method of planting the Wistaria is that the Laburnum is not a very large tree, and after many years' growth does not make a robust-looking trunk as does the Oak, which incidentally would be better able to support the thick woody main stem of an old Wistaria.

This climber is magnificent on a pergola, provided it has good strong stone or brick piers and substantial cross-beams. I have seen it trained on several; the most striking effect was when it was associated with Laburnum: two young trees were planted, one on each side of opposite piers, the upper branches trained over the top to meet in the middle. The thick stems of the Wistaria grew along the horizontal beams and met the Laburnum; the hanging clusters of yellow and lavender flowers being at their best during the first week in June.

In southern gardens the loveliest plant to associate with Wistaria is the rose *R. lutea*, known as the Austrian Briar. It has deep yellow flowers, 3 inches wide, which come in mid-May and continue till the end of June. This rose species needs a warm wall and a limy soil and will make a wonderful patch of yellow by the side of the mauve Wistaria flowers. Another famous climbing yellow Rose is the evergreen *R. banksiae* (the Banksian Rose); the double yellow variety *lutea plena* is the showiest and grows well on trees, pergolas and walls in hot, sunny gardens. It blooms at the end of April and the beginning of May, which may be a little too early for the Wistaria but just right for some of the Clematis: the pink *C. montana rubens*, for instance. Grow it between this pink Clematis and the pale violet variety 'Stella', which is at its best in May. The result is a lovely blending of pink, yellow and violet.

The Honeysuckles bloom at the same time as many of the Climbing Roses we grow in our gardens and both may be planted together over porches or on pergolas. *Lonicera × tellmanniana* is a hybrid Honeysuckle with large trumpet-shaped flowers of a deep yellow, flushed with bronzy-red in the bud, a colour which harmonizes beautifully with pink. The flowers are at their best in most of our gardens about the middle of June, just when the pink-apricot flowers of the climbing 'Albertine' are beginning to show colour. As this Honeysuckle needs shade on its roots and lower stems, it should have some low-growing shrub planted in front of it.

These two climbers give a glorious display of pink and yellow on an old shrub which is not valued for its fruit or its flowers – an old apple bush, for example. Plant the Honeysuckle on the north side of the bush so that its lower stems are shaded from the sun. By the end of June these climbers will be at their best and in a few seasons will cover the top of the bush with flowers.

A more striking effect will be had when these climbers are trained over a large Holly bush, the dark, evergreen leaves showing up the flowers in a remarkable way.

A tall Holly has been used very successfully as a host tree to the charming rose species *R. bracteata* (the Macartney Rose), which has white, scented flowers, 3 inches wide; and the common Honeysuckle of our hedgerows, *Lonicera periclymenum*, with yellowish-white and pink tubular flowers; both planted on the north side of the tree, in shade, and allowed to clamber up into the sun.

The early Dutch Honeysuckle, *L. periclymenum* var. *belgica* is more widely planted and has purplish-red and yellow flowers which look charming with either the pink 'Albertine' or the white Macartney Rose.

Rose species and Honeysuckle are best adapted to growing over tall bushes and trees; they are not always so successful on walls. Some Roses, however, need a warm wall to bring their flowers to perfection. The famous 'Maréchal Niel' (golden-yellow) is on the tender side and mostly grown on walls (when it is not housed) and is a fine companion for some of the deep purple-flowered Clematis. The plants do best on walls facing west.

I have seen this Rose on a west wall and growing with it the plant commonly known as the Everlasting Pea, *Lathyrus pubescens*. Its flowers resemble those of the Sweet Pea (*Lathyrus odoratus*), except that they are smaller and of a thicker texture. The downy *L. pubescens* has violet-pink flowers, carried at the end of stiff, upright stalks, the flowers coming all the way up the main stems, which sometimes reach a height of 20 feet. The one planted with the 'Maréchal Niel' Rose grew 10 feet tall on a wire trellis, which it climbed with the aid of its strong leaf-tendrils. Its mass of violet-pink flowers contrasted well with the golden-yellow flowers of the Rose. The Lathyrus is perennial; its long stems die down during the winter and shoot up again the following spring. It is a vigorous climber mostly used on walls in our gardens, but very effective when it is allowed to scramble over bushes at the back of a sunny border.

There are several forms of this species, which incidentally is a native of Chile and the Argentine. The white-flowered one is particularly beautiful associated with any of the summer-flowering roses. The plants should be set about 4 feet apart.

L. latifolius is another species which is quite common. I have never seen it much above 5 or 6 feet in height. A good way of growing this Everlasting Pea (it has purplish-rose flowers) is to plant several specimens along the wall on which is trained a tall Rose or a Clematis. It is especially useful with the latter, for most of the taller climbing varieties are bare up to about 4 feet of their stems, the flowering shoots coming from the top. The white-flowered *L. latifolius albiflorus* makes a charming companion for the deep purple *Clematis × Jackmanii*. Plant them on a trellis against a west wall and train the slender shoots of the white Lathyrus round the naked stems of the Clematis. Both thrive in ordinary garden soil.

Even more of a dwarf is *L. rotundifolius*, the Persian Everlasting Pea, with bright rose-coloured flowers. An excellent companion for any of the summer-flowering Clematis. It makes a delightful drift of deep rose when it is grown along the base of a wall. I have seen it associated with the paler pink Rose 'Albertine' which, although disappointing on a south wall, often gives a good display on a wall facing west. Toward the end of June both are massed with flowers, the deep pink of the Lathyrus looking very effective below the pink-apricot flowers of the Rose.

The common Sweet-pea is a favourite annual climber. It is sometimes given tall Beech twigs to climb up. I can think of nothing better for it. A clump of a deep pink variety set behind a row of *Salvia × superba (S. virgata nemorosa)*, which has long, slender, purple spikes, is a lovely association. It needs a dark green background: either a closely-clipped Yew hedge or a wall covered with a dark green Ivy; I suggest *Hedera helix*, 'Emerald Green', which has vivid, glossy green leaves.

The evergreen, silver-foliaged wall-shrub *Phlomis fruticosa* (Jerusalem Sage), with its bright yellow flower-heads looks doubly beautiful when planted in conjunction with the purple-pink *Cistus × purpureus*, a hybrid bush rock-rose, evergreen and rather tender in most of our gardens – it is best grown against a wall facing south. With me it succeeds on a sheltered low rockery-wall, which is well protected on the north and east sides by Laurel hedges. The Jerusalem Sage grown with this Cistus makes a delightful association for the summer. There is the contrast in the foliage: the narrow, dull green leaves of the Cistus and the wider, thick, silvery-white leaves of the Phlomis. Then in early summer the yellow and the purple-pink flowers open together. The result is a striking harmony of colour; and diversity is provided by the shapes of the two flowers: erect clusters of yellow and single rose-like, purple-pink ones. The flowers of the Cistus open about midday, when the sun is full on them, and they have fallen by late evening; but the buds come freely and provide a successional display of flowers lasting several weeks.

When these shrubs are planted against a warm wall, as they mostly are, the blue flowers of the Passion Flower, *Passiflora caerulea*, make a lovely background.

Those who have a suitable place for *Cistus × purpureus*, should grow with it a clump of the deep violet-purple *Iris sibirica violacea*, which is a tall, graceful, slender-stemmed perennial, some 5 feet tall; this association is remarkable for its rich colour. Special attention will have to be given to the soil requirements of these two plants: the Cistus flourishes only in poor, sandy soils; and the Iris needs a rich deep moist loam. The latter is easily provided by taking out some of the soil near the shrub (where the Iris is to be planted) and replacing it with a good depth of damp leaf-mould and a little loam. The Iris will grow well in this but would not live long in the shallow soil required by the shrub. The Phlomis also likes a light, sandy soil. (Both shrubs are easily propagated by cuttings; shoots about 4 inches long with a heel should be inserted in sandy soil out of doors and covered with a bell-glass.)

A tall, twining climber which is being more widely planted in our gardens nowadays is *Polygonum baldschuanicum*. It adds much to the beauty of trees like the Poplar, which is uninteresting to many people; but it is rampant and difficult to control on a tall tree, once it reaches the top branches, 40 or 50 feet up. I do not know of any plant which makes such a light, airy mass of blossom as this hardy twiner. When it is trained on a wall, it will want cutting back drastically every year, for it makes 20 feet of growth in a season; if left unpruned, it will soon cover both sides of the wall and smother any climber or wall-shrubs growing near it.

The large-leaved, ornamental Vine *Vitis coignetiae* is a fine climber for a tree (especially attractive on a white-stemmed Birch, as already mentioned); and as a foil to its heavy-looking scarlet leaves, it would be difficult to find anything more suitable than the delicate white and rose-coloured drooping panicles of the Polygonum. Another good companion for it is the equally vigorous *Vitis vitacea* (sometimes called the Common Virginia Creeper – not the true plant) which climbs by means of its twining tendrils and grows as tall as the Polygonum. The leaves of this Vine turn vivid scarlet in late October and give a wonderful glow of colour with the rose-red flowers of the Polygonum. This climber, a native of Turkistan, needs a deep loamy soil.

Some of the most striking plant associations can be had only in the warmest parts of the country. The scarlet-red Pomegranate grown on a wall with the large-flowered, white Clematis 'Henryi' is magnificent in Cornwall but not so successful near London. The Mutisias are also climbers for the warm south and as gorgeous in colour as the Pomegranate. A good place for the tender *Mutisia clematis*, which has brilliant orange-scarlet flowers, is a porch on the south side of a house. I have seen the yellow climbing Rose 'Jersey Beauty' growing with it; the colour association is startling but not objectionable. The best plants to grow with these vividly-coloured Mutisias are the Ceanothus. In the south a blue Ceanothus can be grown in the open garden and one of the orange-coloured Mutisias allowed to ramble through it.

But equally beautiful associations can be had with our popular climbers; and Clematis, Jasmine, Honeysuckle, Roses and Wistaria offer us a wide choice.

BEAN, W. J.	*Trees and Shrubs Hardy in the British Isles.* London.
BEAN, W. J.	*Wall Shrubs and Hardy Climbers.* London.
LAVALLÉE, A.	*Les Clématites à grandes fleurs.* Paris.
MERKHAM, ERNEST.	*Clematis.* London.
REHDER, ALFRED.	*Synopsis of the Genus Lonicera.* St. Louis.
THURSTON, EDGAR.	*Trees and Shrubs in Cornwall.* Cambridge.
WHITEHEAD, STANLEY B.	*Garden Clematis.* London.
WILLMOTT, ELLEN.	*The Genus Rosa.* London.

INDEX